TRUSTED

ANNE DONAHUE

ISBN 978-1-4958-2012-0
eISBN: 978-1-4958-2013-7
Library of Congress Control Number: 2017915023

Published October 2017

INFINITY PUBLISHING
1094 New DeHaven Street, Suite 100
West Conshohocken, PA 19428-2713
Toll-free (877) BUY BOOK
Local Phone (610) 941-9999
Fax (610) 941-9959
Info@buybooksontheweb.com
www.buybooksontheweb.com

DEDICATION

Dedicated to my children

*I loved you even before you were born
I kissed and caressed you with my heart
I sang songs and spoke lovingly to you
While you were still in my womb.*

*I dreamed of a Beautiful Life with you
And I had one-when you were young.*

Authors Note

F irst I would like to ask that you to read this Memoir in an order of sequence, for comprehension of the growth in consciousness, as each chapter unfolds. This book was guided with The Holy Spirit and can surely bring light to those who read it. Often when a person is assaulted, alone and near death, they are protected by a white light or angelic presence in order to survive!

It is my sincere hope that this true story will touch the hearts of physicians, patients, clergy or other people in high power positions! As well, it can benefit those whom have ever been in a physical, emotional, or mentally abusive relationship. I pray that this story will help to enlighten people as to the highly seductive nature of transference and the hypnotic state that it becomes, as though in a trance and unable to break free.

FOREWORD

*"What would happen if one woman told the
truth about her life?
The world would split open."*

*Muriel Rukeyser
(1913–1980), American Poet*

I t is with great honor and pride that I introduce
this compelling true story, **Trusted**, written
by the most significant and influential woman
in my life—my mother, Anne Donahue. Having
experienced this story intimately firsthand from
the perspective of little girl, a young woman, and
a daughter; I have a unique vantage point into the
truth of this story and the impact it has had on
many lives. Now, almost thirty years later and a
therapist myself, I have an even deeper respect for
the courage it has taken my mother to share her
story.

Like many transformative journeys in life,
Trusted is a story of, well, trust...and betrayal.
It is a story about family, religion, the loss of
innocence, and...*love*. It is a story of healing and

forgiveness, and the alchemy of time. It is also a story of power, responsibility and ethics. It is a timepiece and an intimate peek into the life of a woman during the rise of feminism. The raw vulnerability in which Anne bears her heart and soul with us gives us a felt sense of the confusing and often conflicting messages women have been given about our roles in marriage and partnership, motherhood, sexuality, femininity, and our place in the workforce. The most critical aspect of this book, however, is that it is a story about the therapeutic relationship, written from the *client's* experience and understanding.

From a sheltered upbringing of the world as a girl born in the 1950s to a brief teenage marriage and pregnancy in the height of the sexual revolution of the 60s, through the heart-wrenching inner conflict of the taboo of divorce as "good Catholic girl" and the challenge of single motherhood, we feel the naiveté, yet determination that Anne has to create a wholesome life in a rapidly changing world. The influence that media and pop culture has played over time with articles such as "The Good House Wife's Guide" (*Good House Keeping*, 1955) comes screaming out to us through Anne's attempt at understanding "how to be" *for the men* in her life. Even today, we readily see articles in the most popular women's magazines such as "30 Ways to Please Your Man" (*Cosmopolitan, 2014*). We know with anguish Anne's distressing journey to find *Her Self* on her path to emotional, social, and ultimately spiritual maturity.

At a pivotal moment in her life, following a devastating demise of a romantic relationship, she seeks "professional help" with a longtime trusted family psychiatrist. Anne enter into an interpersonal therapeutic relationship that would change the course of her life forever. Demonstrating the profound vulnerability and necessary trust in therapy, she states:

> *"I was hesitant and nervous at pouring out my soul to him and all of the past failures in my life. But I felt that I had no choice at this point. I was ready to mend my life, get some professional help, and grow. And I trusted him implicitly."*

Thus begins the unfolding of the real significance of this story. **Trusted** brings to light the various ways that any healing relationship involving natural power dynamics (client/practitioner, teacher/student, doctor/patient) can fall into the shadows and potentially cause great harm not only to the individual client, but also—through transgenerational impact on others to in the client's life.

"Therapy" often conjures up images of the client lying on a couch with little relational interaction with the therapist. The infamous term "shrink" also denies the vital role of *relating* by implying that the client's mind is altered and "shrunk" by the therapist. As the field of psychology has moved towards a more humanist and client-centered approach, the actual relationship between practitioner and client becomes the container in which profound healing and growth can occur. It is therefore crucial that therapists have an honest understanding of their own projections, blind spots, limits and counter transference in the clinical room, seeking peer guidance and supervision throughout one's career. For it is often in the depths of client transference that clients can overcome relational wounds and traumas that have previously halted the blossoming of a healthy and fulfilling life.

It is my deepest desire that this book, *Trusted*, reaches the hands of many professionals in all of the "helping fields," whether it be psychotherapists, doctors, lawyers, personal trainers, life coaches, teachers, Priests, Shamans, and various other Wisdom keepers. May we remember the power that we hold in these roles with great reverence, and accept that responsibility with integrity and humility. It is truly a gift to touch the life of another and bear witness to the inner life of any human being. It is a gift *to be trusted.*

There are thousands of stories, books, case studies, abstracts, and more about the therapeutic relationship written by practitioners. It is only in reading *Trusted*, however, did I realize that I had only read one book in my clinical education written from a *client's perspective*, and yet this client was also a therapist herself. Practitioners need to hear more unfiltered stories of clients' experience of the therapeutic relationship. This is the true brilliance and gift of *Trusted.* We bear witness to the beautiful and often excruciating path of becoming *Oneself* within the multiple therapeutic encounters; some harming, some healing.

By the end of the story we have been transported through time, heartbreaks, failures and triumphs, and ultimately we have the privilege to know the process of a girl becoming a woman, becoming her own teacher and guide, and developing the most vital relationship of all; one with herself and God.

For all of you who have ever felt broken, lost and betrayed, may **Trusted** be a beacon of light on your path in your own journey to wholeness. And while it is crucial for each of us to seek the reflection and comfort of others to walk with us, may we also remember to always come back to our own hearts and look within, and to know the essence of Spirit that is available to us all.

People often ask me how my mother's experience has influenced my life as a practitioner. I admit I grew up with a fierce determination to avoid being naïve, vulnerable, and even loved at all costs. I had a severe distrust of Western medicine and the masculine in general. The beautiful unexpected consequence of that was that I spent my developing years exploring other ways of "healing" and knowing, such as world religions, alternative and ancient medicines, Eastern traditions and other cultures, the healing ways of women before science, and I even had the profound blessing of having two home births. And here I am with degrees from the finest universities and wisdom from all sorts of traditions and modalities, having learned how to truly integrate it all. For this, I am eternally grateful to my mother, Anne Donahue, for walking her path as it encouraged me to trailblaze my own.

I bow down with respect and awe to my mother. She has shown me what gentle strength and endurance is. She has shown what it is to fall down and what it is to rise. Through my mother I have learned compassion, forgiveness, sweetness, playfulness, purity, innocence and grace. She has shown me what it is to know God and walk with Spirit guiding our lives. She is my best friend and we have learned to laugh and play together with a cherished knowing that ultimately, all is well.

> *It's not too difficult to get the skeletons out of the closet with people, but to get the gold out is a different matter. That is therapy. Psychology is the Art of finding the gold of the spirit.*
>
> **Robert Johnson, Jungian Analyst**
>
> *There are many ways of healing and many paths to wholeness, all leading to the same place. We are all interconnected and always with Spirit.*

Nadine Keller, MA

Integrative Holistic Practitioner
Ordained Priestess Minister

Half Moon Bay, California 2017

TRUSTED

CHAPTER 1

How It Began

Flashback

The waves gently caressed my naked body as I drifted out to the ocean under the dark blue moon and starlit night. If I were going to die, this would be the best way to go — slowly and quietly under the heavens and into the sea. But I found myself back on the sandy shore, as if pulled in the opposite direction by some external force beyond my control, like the way he silently seduced me for so many years in the secret confines of his office!

I awakened shivering once again to the same nightmare that I had been having for years now. *When would it end?* I thought. *When would the pain go away, and when would I be healed and feel whole again, like the woman I had been* — the wonderful mother that I thought I was, a doctor's daughter, and a nurse. *When, oh when, would my identity return and my heart heal from the painful memories of the years he had mentally entrapped me while assaulting me!*

My Mother's Doctor

It was my mother who introduced me to Dr. Paul Brady in 1970, during part of my rebel years. She was his patient and thought the world of him! "He is so handsome, intelligent, and charming," she often would day. "A stable man, too," she surmised. The psychiatrist was also married with four children. I suppose that gave him a "blue ribbon" in her eyes as well. She had been seeing him for many years. It seemed he was almost part of our family, listening to her. And she would frequently refer to him jokingly as her "boyfriend"!

Although I was reluctant she finally convinced me to see him, as I had told her that I was going to leave my husband. "This was not part of your Catholic upbringing, to get a divorce!" she emphatically would say. So she made an appointment for me.

The Psychiatrist

I still remember what I was wearing the hot summer day I met him at his hospital office in San Diego. It was my favorite long multicolored polka dot dress, symbolic of the Hippie Era. I had taken it from a store with my girlfriend.

When the nurse took me back to his office, I blushed upon meeting him. Dr. Brady greeted me with a big smile and gentle handshake. He was small in stature but very handsome with a Southern California tan face, sandy colored hair, and deep blue eyes. I imagined that he probably played golf or tennis.

He wore a taupe-colored suit and a torques tie. Silver glasses fell partially down his small nose. He was seventeen years my senior.

Nervously I sat down across from him. Having never been with this kind of a doctor before, I didn't really know what to expect. I began pulling on my long blond hair, as was my habit when apprehensive. He seemed to be intensely staring into my green eyes in what felt like an eternity.

Then finally, while crossing his legs, he began to speak.

"I know your mother well, Anne. She is a very nice person. I'll be happy to see you."

"Oh," I stammered, "I'm not sure why I am here...?"

With that he encouraged me to tell him about myself and what was going on in my life.

I slowly began to explain that my marriage was in turmoil. I was twenty years old with a nine-month-old baby girl, named Nadine, and didn't care anymore if I left my husband, Jay. I thought it would be for our own good, as he was using drugs, drinking, and had dropped out of college with no promise of a decent career.

I then looked up at Dr. Brady embarrassingly while explaining to him, "I had run away from home just before high school graduation, but I did get my diploma." I quickly added, "And I am now trying to patch things up with my family. However, my mother didn't approve of divorce and wanted me to see you for advice!"

He asked how my husband was treating me.

I cautiously began explaining that money was hard, as Jay only worked part time at a gas station. "He had hit me a couple times and even pulled a knife out once while yelling at me.

"I locked myself in the bathroom as he cut apart my favorite painting on our wall. It was a beautiful nude lady in a garden." I wondered if he imagined it was me.

Dr. Brady's face turned very serious and he seemed to be thinking deeply about something while taking notes.

Then with his gentle prompting I slowly continued to speak, though I was unable to look him in the eyes.

"We live in Ocean Beach, but I am thinking of moving to Encinitas, where I will be closer to my family and could get a job. It was pretty wild where we lived," I explained. I was in a hippie area with parties and drugs and I didn't feel safe there anymore especially with Nadine. Hesitantly I continued to explain that I could not share my pregnancy with my husband. It made him very uncomfortable. I felt like he is not much of a family man.

"How did you meet him, Anne?" he queried.

I told him that we had met in my third year of high school. I was in a Catholic girls' school and Jay had been in my older brother's circle of friends. Most of the other boys had gone off to Vietnam. As I was having trouble at home and my parents wanted to send me back East to live with some relatives, I ran away with him. He was a "conscientious objector" of the war, and I respected that!

I told him how we went to Mexico first for two weeks but our car broke down. We got a ride from some local guys to take us to our hotel, but they passed it and when Jay yelled to stop, one pulled out a knife and told us to be quiet. When I told Jay to shush they stopped the car, laughing. We quickly started to get out, but one of them yanked me by my panties as I was leaving the car. I was really scared but I made it out with Jay pulling me. Then we ran as fast as we could! Returning to Oceanside we found a little house where Jay had grown up, then married right after summer.

After a long pause, Dr. Brady stared at me intently while saying, "Anne, this is sad for you and I am so sorry. You are so young and beautiful and you deserve better!" I could feel my face turning red over what he said, and I really didn't feel beautiful!

I was tired now, as though unable to continue too much longer. I think that he could see it in my eyes. With his sweet smile he quietly asked if I could come to his La Jolla office next week, and there we could talk some more and that he would like to help me. I agreed that I would come as he was a fine gentleman and seemed to like me too, which made me feel safe and good.

His La Jolla Office

Nestled behind tiny stores and overlooking the beautiful Pacific Ocean above La Jolla cove was Dr. Brady's office. I had been on Prospect Street before but never really noticed this hidden place.

There was a large white gate covered with pretty vines of lavender and yellow emitting a lovely sweet scent. I knew that it was a very wealthy area. My mother loved to shop here and as a child we would come to a fine restaurant nearby, called Mrs. B's.

Opening the tall iron gate, I came upon an enclosed brick patio surrounded by pretty tropical plants, which stirred up a cozy feeling. It was the only office there. His waiting room felt comfortable, with brown and beige colors and some natural ocean artifacts placed near the wooden tables and sofa. On the wall hung several lovely ocean oil paintings.

It didn't feel like a regular doctor's waiting room at all. In fact it was very quiet, like a library. Definitely an improvement over his small hospital office. His secretary greeted me with friendliness as well.

Before long a side door opened and Dr. Brady called my name, summoning me back with a gentle voice and warm smile. I followed him back to his private counseling room, remembering that this was where my mother had been seeing him for years! He offered me the beige leather sofa while he sat across from me on an office chair beside a handsome walnut desk covered with papers.

There was a huge glass window with a spectacular view of the brilliant blue ocean; it hung over the cove and seemed never-ending. One could even see Catalina Island from it. Seagulls flew by and there were several sailboats on the water too! White older homes cascaded down moss and flower-covered hills, ending at La Jolla shores. It was so surreal it took my breath away and gave me a warm and wonderful feeling of life and beauty here in Southern California.

Beginning Counseling

I sat there quietly not knowing what to say and wondering why I was there this time. Dr. Brady asked me how I was doing and I nodded okay, with a smile. Then he took the lead, asking me to tell him about my childhood. I proceeded by telling him that I was from a large Catholic family as he knew, and that at times it had been very hard. There were a lot of rules to follow and my parents often argued about money. But we also had a lot of fun together.

He suddenly asked me: "Do you remember ever being held when you were young?"

I didn't really understand the significance of this and had to think about it for a while.

Then I replied: "Well, no not really, but there were so many of us. I am sure, though, that I was held as a baby!" and I added with pride that, "I also helped out a lot with the younger five children too." I was the third oldest.

"I see," he said, while making notes in his chart. Then he looked up at me and wanted to know what books I was interested in. I said shyly that I like books about nutrition, psychology, and nature. I was reading a book then called: *I Never Promised You a Rose Garden*. He said he knew the book: "It was about a mother who had mental illness and was not nice to her daughter. It was sad but deep, with so much meaning about life and how to overcome obstacles and lack of love."

"Oh, yes," I replied, loving that he too knew the story and I added that I loved books by David Thoreau and Ralph Waldo Emerson too!

"Anne," he responded, "these are good books. They show your interest in human nature and that you are a caring individual!" Then he asked: "Have you considered a career in a particular field?"

"Yes, I said, "I wanted to be a nurse when I was younger but now I have a baby and all I can do and want to do now is to take care of her!"

He answered, "Well, that is admirable!"

At times I became very quiet not knowing what I was supposed to say or do. He said I could talk about anything I wanted to, but I wasn't used to being expressive about my feelings or taking the lead. He suggested that I keep a journal of my dreams and that we could talk about them for our next visit. It was nice, I thought, to be able to have someone to share my personal interests with and that It was acceptable.

On my third visit I had told him that I was already separated from my husband. Dr. Brady thought it was in the best interest at this time for us. We then went on to discuss more about my husband who had come from a broken home and had a mentally ill mother.

"He was very bossy to me and I had to work part time to make ends meet," I told him. Dr. Brady thought it would be a good idea to meet Jay for an assessment of our situation.

When he asked me about my dream journal, I began to blush. I could barely tell him my first dream. But he coaxed me while assuring me that "everything was confidential and there was no need to be embarrassed about anything here. You can trust me, Anne." With my heart throbbing, I bravely told him about a sexual dream I had about a man seducing me. Then I quickly added another one about running away from an orphanage.

He slowly took off his glasses, wiping them with a cloth, and staring right at me he asked, "Anne, do you think men like you just for sex and do you feel this is the main relationship between you and men?"

"I suppose that I do because I went to an all-girls school." He then asked me how many relationships I had with men in the past. "What do you mean?" I stammered.

"Sexual," he replied.

"Well, I had about four experiences with boys before I was married," I replied.

He continued: "Do you see anything wrong with this, Anne?"

"No," I said, "I don't." It was of course the era of free love, I thought, and smiled at him.

The next visit I wasn't there. My husband had agreed to go in to see him. I don't know what they discussed with each other that day, but the next time I saw Dr. Brady he said to me that he did not think my husband was emotionally stable enough to be a family man. This cemented what I had felt and gave me the strength to begin divorce proceedings a few weeks later, despite what my family thought.

I did go to see Dr. Brady a couple of more times to tell him what had developed. He asked me what the reason was, why I finally divorced my husband. I explained that it just hit me one day that it was not a healthy marriage and that I needed to move on and to protect my little girl.

CHAPTER 2

AS A YOUNG WOMAN

My Youth

It was a couple of years before I saw Dr. Brady again. There seemed to be no reason to go back once I was divorced. I was very busy raising my daughter and working at the new May Company Department store. Luckily I did have my family to help me out and life went on.

Nadine, my daughter, was now three years old and we were very close. We traveled across the country together visiting relatives in Connecticut. In the summers we went to Lake Tahoe with my family on vacations. And she enjoyed playing at Grandma and Grandpa's home with their beautiful yard and pool. We loved to garden together, juice, and cook. It was a very happy time in our lives.

My High School Sweetheart

My high school sweetheart Josh, who had been in Vietnam, called to ask me to come and live with him in Northern California, near Lake Tahoe. Although hesitant, due to family rules as well as my divorce, I did go for a visit to see how Nadine and I would like it.

It was the most beautiful time in my life! We were there for the first snowfall in November. I loved wearing boots and being only one hour from Lake Tahoe and seeing the beautiful countryside. Josh lived in a small cabin on a river surrounded by huge pine trees. We laughed together, made love, and went to a small country fair with Josh holding Nadine on his shoulders. I also met some of his friends and family. I had freedom that I had never known before. I was twenty-three years old.

Although I wanted to stay with him, something about it scared me. For one thing, I felt that I would be letting my family down once again. Plus, I had only been divorced for one year, which made me hesitant. I know how sad Josh was when I told him that I had to go back home. He had loved me since we were sixteen, before my marriage.

Still I remembered our first kiss.

We had gone walking then on a Sunday afternoon in Carlsbad. He held my hand while leading me down the hillside near the railroad tracks, which were right across from the ocean. Josh was fascinated with trains! Sitting on a large rock beside the tracks, we began to hug and kiss one another. It seemed as if we were the only two people in the universe at that moment!

Another year passed before I saw Josh again. He was passing through town while returning from a motorcycle trip with my older brother, who lived with us. It was late in the evening when they arrived. We all had a nice visit and when I was alone with Josh, we couldn't help but become romantic again. He was such a fun and loving person to be around and we were overcome with passion.

The next morning Josh left, and two weeks later I suspected I might be pregnant. I had attempted some old-fashioned birth control but I now was feeling changes in my body, which were verified a couple of weeks later. When my brother mentioned that Josh had been dating a girl in his hometown I felt betrayed. We had been friends for many years.

By the tone of my voice Josh seemed to know right away why I was calling. He asked me if I wanted to get married but I replied angrily: "No I don't!" and told him I heard he was seeing someone. Then I hung up the phone. Truly I just didn't like the way he had asked me to marry him and now I did not trust him!

I had begun nursing school, but now pregnant I did not know what to do! When I told my parents they were very dismayed: they didn't approve of Josh, but they never seemed to like anyone their daughters dated back then. I suppose being strict Catholics, they were just being overprotective. My father still wanted me to finish nursing school, telling me, "You will need to support your family."

In my eyes abortion was not an option, even though it had become legal that year on January 22, 1973. I knew within my soul and my feminine spirit, as a woman, that it just was not the right thing to do. This was a child I held within me, and motherhood meant the world to me! It was what I dreamed of. But I was naïve as to all of the responsibilities of raising a family alone.

When I was three months pregnant, I went up north to see Josh. I was already in love with the baby and felt myself blossoming once again. I always felt the first flutters of movement within my womb early on. It was like a butterfly softly and gently caressing me!

I found Josh with the help of his friends. He was living in a small trailer on some beautiful land then, closer to his family's home. It was a surprise visit. When I told him that I could already feel the baby he was amazed. He also seemed quiet and standoffish. I only remember that I started to cry because he seemed so distant! I thought he would be happy like me, but I believe he was probably fearful of the reality of it all. I left his trailer feeling very upset.

On My Own

After I returned home, I knew that I had to make it on my own now. I kept my sales job at the department store but felt it was too much to continue my nursing studies. Before long I began to work at my father's medical office. The months flew by!

Unknown to me, my parents had arranged for a family back East to adopt my baby! One day while in their bedroom, I saw the letter from the couple thanking them for this chance to have a baby. Horrified, I ran from my parents' home, asserting, "I would not give my baby up!"

Dr. Brady was the one I needed to see. The person you went to when you had a problem. I felt so alone in the world. When he returned my phone call, I asked if I could see him while trying to hold back my tears. He immediately asked what was wrong and if I wanted to talk. Bursting into tears, I told him that I was six months pregnant! He replied, "Well it's too late to do anything about it, but come in to see me and we will talk." It occurred to me that he may have been thinking about abortion, but I put it out of my mind!

I arrived at Dr. Brady's office wearing the black velvet maternity dress that my mother had given me. Even though it was already spring, I loved the pretty dress and wanted to look nice.

"Well," he said immediately and with his friendly smile, "it is obvious that you are expecting," and "you look very lovely." I smiled a little while blushing.

Shyly I explained about my relationship with Josh and what had occurred between us. When I told him that I wasn't sure of marriage, he responded that perhaps I should think about it as it is hard to raise children alone. Otherwise it would be to my benefit to get some kind of license for the future in order to handle financial responsibilities. "Well," I replied, "I just want to be a mother and take care of my children, but I don't see how I could go back to school!"

"Anyway," I continued, "I am now working in my father's office and enjoyed that very much. It is the receptionist and billing job. After the baby is born, perhaps I would be able to advance."

"That is good for now of course, Anne, and I'll be happy to see you during this challenging time," he assured me.

My Love Baby

I continued to work in my father's office until my baby was born. I named him Sean, which meant "God's Grace." Nadine's name meant "hope." Nadine just adored her new baby brother. "He is my little doll," she would say. My whole family of ten, including Great Grandma, loved my new infant, as they did Nadine. They were all mesmerized by another beautiful child in our lives. Sean had Josh's bright blue eyes and my blonde hair. There was nothing like a new wonderful life to cherish and bring happiness and hope to everyone. Mother even said that I should have named him Josh, which baffled me as I didn't think she like him!

Not long after Sean's birth, I received a message from my father that Josh had phoned for me at their home. I had mailed him a beautiful photo of Sean, but we had just moved and he did not know how to contact me. Dad didn't sound very pleasant when he told me about Josh, and I didn't realize that he was in town. I never called him back as I hadn't heard from him and assumed he was probably married. I did find out later, though, from his sister, that he had waited by the phone all day before returning to his home in Northern California!

When Sean was a few months old, Josh asked us to come up to visit. He was married now and lived near San Francisco. As soon as we got off the train, he grabbed his baby son and held him in his arms. He was so happy and so was I to see this.

His wife was expecting their first child. She was accepting of us but a little distant too, I felt. We visited for the weekend going to the San Francisco Zoo like a family, and I so hated to leave! But Josh said that we would stay in touch now.

Upon returning home, I signed up for Medical Assisting College with my father's advice. By the time Sean was two years old I had graduated. I truly enjoyed working with patients, my father, and being a mother too, of course! For now it seemed like a solid life for me. At times, though, I did wonder if I could ever meet another man whom I could fall in love with!

CHAPTER 3

RECURRING ISSUES

Visiting Josh

There was no time to date for me. I was a busy single mother—and I still felt connected to Josh. I felt committed to him because I bore his child and still thought someday we would be a couple. I also was skeptical of other men as stepfathers. I wanted to protect my children from any possibility of harm, whether through an unhappy marriage or by being a victim of some kind.

In the autumn of 1977, when Sean was two-and-a-half years old, Josh wanted us to come visit again. He actually was hoping that we would move beside them into another trailer. They were now living in Nevada, where he continued advancing his career as a railroad engineer. The children and I flew over to see them and were able to stay in their home.

On the flight over, I began to reminisce of fond teenage memories with Josh—of our high school dance, family outings, and our first kiss! He often came to visit me on his own with no car, while not accepting a ride back home due to his pride. Sometimes we would go to the local drag races in Carlsbad, and loved our local A&W root beer drive-through for lunch. Those were such simple and enjoyable times together, which seemed so short-lived now!

After landing in Nevada, we were all greeted with warmth. Josh was always very loving to us all! To my great surprise, though, Josh's wife had set me up with a date to see if we might like each other. It was in hopes that we could move there so Josh could be near Sean, Nadine, and me. By now they had their own baby boy! But I felt uncomfortable with the man on the date and with all of the arrangements!

Somewhere inside of me it didn't feel right. The third evening we were all in their living room and tension began mounting with Josh's wife. I insisted then to go to a hotel and fly back home the following morning!

It Happened Again

While driving to the hotel, Josh apologized for the situation, saying that it was difficult having two women under the same roof. I expressed the same sentiments. Upon entering my hotel room, suddenly Josh pulled me into the bathroom while the children were playing. We smothered each other with kisses while stripping off our clothes! He had me up against the wall, and we were hardly able to catch our breath! I was so lonely and yearning to be with him too, he was such a good man and lover and father of our baby! It was impossible to stop, nor did I want to!

Two weeks later, back home while taking a bath, I had sudden cramps in my abdomen. I suddenly suspected, with shock, that I might be pregnant again. It just didn't seem possible that this could happen again, after having sex only two times in five years! I was still breastfeeding Sean, which was supposed to be a contraceptive as well!

But my suspicion was confirmed a couple of weeks later. My family doctor called me to give me the positive report. I began weeping, knowing that Josh was married and wondering what to do now. My doctor said it was not his place to decide morals. Hanging up the phone, I was wishing that he could have coaxed me more. I only imagined how furious my folks would be. As well, I did not want to break up Josh's marriage, no matter how much I loved him!

Lying in the tub that evening, I felt in awe once again at being a mother, carrying his baby and bringing a new life into the world. The life and spirit in my womb was ours and God's, I thought! Slowly, though, my nervousness overtook me, and I made a quick decision this time to have an abortion.

Years later my sister and I would weep over this together. It was not what I believed in, but I was so afraid to confront anyone! With my sister by my side we went to a clinic, thinking it was a very early on pregnancy and, this way, no one would know what had happened. It all went so fast; it was a cold atmosphere and routine, as though just getting a pap smear and you were done!

Shortly after, I began to remember my project in Medical Assisting College. I had brought an embryo of a tiny baby still within a uterus preserved in glass. Dad was able to borrow it from the hospital lab for my project on abortion. Everyone in class was astonished at the beauty and perfection of the teeny tiny baby nestled within the womb! I received an A+ on my report. Some students came up to me saying they never would have had an abortion if they had known this was such a well-developed baby even at six weeks!

Depression set in after the abortion and loss of my child. The shock to my body, mind and spirit was overwhelming. Although hidden, I knew in my heart what had happened and that I had gone against my true feelings of love and womanhood! I then was prescribed an antidepressant for the next two years.

I couldn't help but wonder how odd it was in the Church to be reprimanded for being unmarried and pregnant, but then it was bad to have an abortion too! Somehow it seemed you were damned if you do and damned if you don't! It made me feel confused for being me and for wanting to *be loved*!

It seemed pointless to see Dr. Brady this time as I was ashamed. I simply took care of my children and worked while keeping to myself. Over the next two years I gained 30 lbs. and finally decided to mail the lab report of the pregnancy and abortion to Josh, due to my guilt.

The whole incident was very disruptive to all of us. Josh told me that I should not have had the abortion! Inside of me I thought I had done it for their sake and others, but I also had felt angry and abandoned in some way and I wanted them to know!

It ended our relationships permanently. I know Josh had to make a decision not to see us again because of his wife, and she threatened to take Sean away from me too! It frightened me so much that I decided never to contact them again!

However, it did heal something in me by telling them! I lost the weight and was able to discontinue the antidepressant and begin over again.

Dr. Brady's Support

Off and on over several years I went to visit Dr. Brady for counseling. I knew my mother was still seeing him too, as it was the thing to do then when one had a problem. I would simply go in for support as a single parent. He was a doctor whom I truly trusted and could speak to about my life and family issues. "I can't seem to break away completely and move on with my own life," I explained to him one day.

Dr. Brady would remind me how difficult it was to be single with two children and meet a man.

He confided in me some personal things about my mother, often reminding me of her inadequacies, "being emotionally distant sometimes, strict, and overzealous about religion and morals!" He added that he would just "listen to her ventilate" when she came in to see him! I was aware that I often had a different point of view from mom's—and we did have arguments through the years it was true.

Sometimes I would just leave Dr. Brady's office feeling sad with no desire to return. What lifted me up were my two beautiful children, and we had a pretty good life together. At this time, they were the focus of my life. I imagined that it would be nice to have a mate, but I pushed it aside for the time being.

CHAPTER 4

NEW LOVE

Romance

Three years flew by and I did in fact fall deeply in love again at the age of twenty-nine.

Chad was the handsome Irish son of my parents' best friends. He had been divorced for six months. Upon our first meeting at his parents' home, his dark eyes widened and a large smile came over his inquisitive face. I was wearing a soft white knit sweater with a matching skirt. He seemed to be glaring at me, making me feel a bit standoffish. I knew I really needed time to get to know a man then.

Chad was very sensitive, funny, and good with my children. He often did impressions of Donald Duck, tickled them, and was fantastic at other games as well. It was obvious that they were very fond of him, too. He was a natural family man who had a Catholic background and four siblings. We spent every weekend together taking pictures, laughing, and sharing lovely outings with each other. From the beginning of our relationship Chad seemed enchanted with me, and within a few weeks I had fallen in love with him too. He was thirty-one and I was twenty-nine.

Making love with him was beautiful, touching my heart and soul! Sometimes we would enjoy it under the moon and stars in my backyard! I could feel we were becoming more and more like a true family. Most nights he would telephone me just to chat and find out how my day had gone! His parents and mine were ecstatic! Everyone assumed we would be engaged before long. My mother even bought a lovely cream-colored lace nightgown for me, right after Chad had given me a heart necklace.

Everything seemed to be falling into place. I felt this was real and that we truly were in love. It had been many years since I felt this kind of love, and I began to realize that true happiness was possible as a wife, mother, and woman! It was all so deeply close, beautiful, and nurturing!

As we were becoming more serious, we decided it would be wise to use birth control. Having simply fallen head over heels with one another, we now had to plan. But a week later I discovered I was already pregnant!

Although it was a huge surprise, I was very happy as I assumed we would be married soon anyway! I was glowing with happiness and filled with love, often admiring my already blooming body in the mirror with awe. I imagined myself six months pregnant while placing my hand gently over my tummy, extending my blouse out and looking so beautiful! It would be wonderful to continue a family with Chad. Nadine and I even went searching for a lovely lace wedding dress!

Disbelief

When I contemplated telling Chad that I was pregnant, I suddenly became scared while remembering some of my difficult past. After he phoned one night, I became very quiet. He had to ask me several questions before the truth was finally revealed! I immediately expressed my joy and happiness to him but to my shock, he retorted, "Happy? How could you be happy — we have only been dating a few months!" He added, "I am not sure I am ready to take care of a family of three children! My parents, being Catholic, will be shocked and so will yours!" he explained.

"Well, it just feels natural to be happy, Chad, when you are in love and pregnant!" I responded.

With that he decided to come over and discuss this on the weekend, saying that he needed time to think things over. Now I felt very awkward and saddened that he did not feel the same way I did.

I could not believe what I heard. I thought he loved me and my children! Underneath I was feeling distrustful of him and was not sure I could believe anything he would say again! On the weekend we held each other in a long embrace on the sofa, just feeling tenderness and warmth towards one another. He softly said that it felt different this time to be near me knowing that I was pregnant!

Chad told me that he was considering moving closer to us, buying a home, and getting married. But I could see in his heart that he was not really ready for all of this. Then he suggested that I could have an abortion and we could plan a baby later after we were married. "That way our parents would not find out what had happened," he explained.

My fear of losing Chad, while feeling confused then, made me go along with him. I had the abortion at ten weeks along. Afterwards, though, nothing felt the same with our relationship. Once again I became very depressed and now unable to communicate with him. I pretended that it was all right, it had happened before.

A few weeks later Chad called me to say, "We should not see each other anymore. We don't communicate well and it was the baby that kept us together."

"I thought you loved me, Chad?" I asked.

"I don't anymore!" came his reply.

With this I began sinking to the kitchen floor wanting to die, as he continued saying in a monotone voice, "I am regrouping and was on a rebound from my previous marriage too!" But I would find out, years later, that this was not all true!

My head was whirling as my dreams of a beautiful wedding and marriage came crashing all around me, along with my thoughts of more children and being a part of him and his wonderful family too. I was so sure I had finally found the perfect mate after so many years on my own. I was in shock and felt so abandoned! Terrible grief descended on me for the loss of the baby and now Chad!

Emotional Loss

I swore I would never date another man under forty years of age! As everything that had happened played in my mind over the next few weeks, I lost 20 pounds while sinking into yet another depression.

Sleep was impossible. I felt so helpless, dark circles started to appear under my eyes. People who saw me would ask what was wrong. Even the patients were worried about me but I said nothing. Barely able to get through the days, I would suddenly leave Dad's office without saying a word and go home. I closed my curtains for weeks, staying in bed.

My parents would come to visit bringing food and trying to cheer me up, but I just felt immobile! No one really knew of all the intimate circumstances. I was alone in my depression, unable to bare my soul to anyone.

My mother, knowing how much I loved Chad and also wanting this for me, suggested I could get pregnant! To myself I thought I had been honest, which was supposed to be the right way. Little did she know this had already happened! One day at lunch she said that she'd like to write a book about my life. I could only think, for some reason, that she might be the highlight of it. We had had a stormy relationship, and I didn't always trust her amid all the mishaps that had occurred in my life.

I contemplated suicide, but knew it was not possible due to the deep love and bond I had with my two children! I tried to contact Chad and to recapture what we had lost but it didn't work.

One day I was so overwrought with life that I started to scream. This prompted me to make an appointment with Dr. Brady again, as I had to get my life straightened out. It was necessary to be there for my children as well, and to understand what was happening and why I continued to fail at relationships!

CHAPTER 5

CONSISTENT THERAPY

My inner Wounds

U pon returning to Dr. Brady, I opened up my heart to him as to what had occurred with Chad and the terrible ending, even telling him about the abortion. At first I was hesitant and nervous at pouring out my soul to him and all of the past failures in my life, but I felt that I had no choice at this point. I was ready to mend my life, get some professional help, and grow. And I trusted him implicitly.

Dr. Brady was compassionate, as though holding me with his loving spirit. He was not judgmental at all. He even said, "Having an abortion is the time a woman needs to be held and not abandoned!" At hearing this, I thought that he was a very sensitive and understanding man. I could never tell my parents about such things!

"Have you fully grieved the loss of the baby, as well as Chad?" Dr. Brady asked.

"Yes, I must have, and now I feel as though I had hit rock bottom!" I replied. "Now I just feel distracted with difficulty sleeping." I did not comprehend the full depth of grief, but knew about depression.

"You need to be treated with kid gloves, Anne," Dr. Brady said then.

At the end of the session he said, "You have really reached your limit in life, Anne. I would like to see you weekly now to build a relationship with you, so that I can determine your ups and downs and gather more information."

I was only too eager to get started then. He prescribed an antidepressant, Desyrel, and a tranquilizer, Stelazine, to help me get through this difficult time. He said that I should take them every morning like vitamins.

I was now thirty years old, and Dr. Brady mentioned that this was the first time that I seemed like an adult. He also noted how I seemed to able to share my feelings freely with maturity at this time. It seemed the trauma had awakened me to my own needs and possible potential.

For the next four months I saw Dr. Brady every week. We went over more details of my family background, such as how all of the extreme Catholic discipline may have attributed to some of my behavior and low self-esteem. He thought, too, that my mother was jealous of me and projected

"Marilyn Monroe" onto me as well. I didn't think a mother could be jealous of her daughter, but I just listened.

Dr. Brady also spoke to me about developing my own identity and values! I wasn't really sure what he meant. I just knew about being a mother and nurse. I did share, though, that I pondered the idea of going back to college to become a psychologist. He did not think it was a lucrative enough career for a woman; he thought there were so many of them out there!

At the end of sessions, I noticed that he would lock my chart in his desk drawer after we were finished. Well, it was the thing to do, I presumed, for privacy.

Building Trust

Every week I became more accepting and trusting of Dr. Brady. I began to understand that I had a life of my own to live and that it did not apply to my family or past. Dr. Brady, having met Chad once when I was trying to mend things, did not really think he was as wonderful as I thought him to be. He said he may know computers, but that he did not seem so extraordinary. But to me, I thought he was ideal in the ways that I had needed!

I did ask Dr. Brady, "What do men want to talk about with women anyway?"

He gave me a big smile while saying, "Just everyday things, Anne, like my mother makes the best apple pie in the world!" We both began laughing then.

I supposed that I was not as knowing about men because I had gone to an all-girls Catholic school. I reminisced that I had three brothers who were related to me but somehow I felt shyness around other men.

My appointments were scheduled the last of the day. Dr. Brady had expressed to me, "It makes my day when I know that you are coming in, Anne. I look forward to our visits!" That made me feel very happy and special! He asked me once how I felt about relationships: "Are you a one-man woman, or do you prefer seeing several men?"

I was a bit baffled but I strongly replied, "Oh, no, I am a one-man-only woman. I want one special relationship!"

Unconsciously I was holding my blue sweater over my breasts as he spoke. He brought it to my attention, saying, "Your body language is telling me how shy you are." I immediately dropped the sweater, giggling at my silliness covering myself up!

Then he told me I had a lot to offer a man— that men would be attracted to me because of my femininity and beauty.

"I thought all women were feminine?" I asked.

"Oh no, Anne," he replied, "they are not! You are beautiful, soft and caring, a mother, and a doctor's daughter. Don't you realize how important this is to a man?" He continued, "You mentioned that you did not go to a traditional college, just a vocational school."

"Yes," I responded.

"But this is not the main asset in a good relationship," he assured me.

I was beginning to feel better with these visits. I was even gaining a little weight back. My self-esteem had improved and I was connecting with my children again on a deeper level. They were always my angels! However, I was a bit tired and spacey from the medicines. But I did not want to be depressed anymore, so continued on them as he advised me.

Bonding

On one of my visits, Dr. Brady began to speak first. He seemed to have something on his mind.

"If only you knew, Anne, just how special you are. I would like to take your hand and walk and talk with you outdoors, if this would make you feel more comfortable." I wasn't sure what he meant. Then he continued: "I think there were a couple of times when you were here in the past when you felt that I might be interested in you, were there?" he asked, as my face turned Crimson.

I slowly answered, "Well, maybe…."

"Yes!" was his emphatic response, "And I think that we felt a connection the first time we met."

I remembered at nineteen feeling this connection with him. I smiled at the memory while nodding my head yes.

"I am divorced now," he said, and my eyes widened with surprise. He continued, "I know only too well the heartaches of relationships. I thought maybe I could help you bond with a man in this safe environment. I know it has been difficult for you, Anne, and that you need to be handled with kid gloves. I hate to see you live your life without knowing this special bonding of a man and a woman."

I trusted him as a psychiatrist and felt safe opening up to him as well now, especially these last few months. He did seem almost a part of the family. He was still treating my mother and had seen my two sisters briefly. My father had even gone in to visit him once to ask his advice about some marriage and money issues. Dr. Brady had shared with me that he had suggested to my father that when my mother gave too many expensive gifts to the family, he should quietly ask them to return the gifts. And now I felt especially close to Dr. Brady! He was sharing confidential things with me, too.

Suddenly Dr. Brady leaned toward me, smiling, and asked, "Anne, would you like me to hold you?"

I was rather taken aback with the question, but softly and slowly found myself whispering, "Yes...!"

"Can I come over to the sofa and put my arms around you?" and he continued, "Only if this is what you want, Anne, because sometimes I feel that it is."

It was true that I had felt affection toward him for a long time. Once again he had helped me through another very painful time and understood so much about my life and family, too.

I began to remember the time my mother was telling me what an intelligent doctor he was and I had responded, "He has a good bod too, Mom." Then we both laughed. It was all in jest, but my mom had mentioned it to him.

Now with longing in my eyes I excitedly replied again, "Yes, you could sit by me and I would like to be held!" With this he came over to the sofa where I had been sitting across from him for so many years!

He slowly sat down beside me and tenderly wrapped his arms around me. The first thing I said was, *"I feel like a little girl!"*

Dr. Brady warmly replied with a softness in his eyes, "You needed to be held for some time, Anne, and it feels so wonderful."

It seemed I had done so much work all my life for family and others and expected nothing in return, I was thinking. And now I was feeling very needy and it truly did feel safe and so special to be in his loving arms. He told me I was "like a kitten, loving to be caressed, snuggled, and touched" and he loved doing it. I felt safe and secure in his arms too!

My head was on his shoulder and I was staring at his strong hand with the nice golden watch on it. That always made me feel good about a man. There is a certain strength in men's hands! Then as I gazed into his eyes our lips suddenly touched, and we became locked in a passionate kiss which seemed to last forever! All these years of trials and always having him to turn to — my breath was heavy and so was his.

We automatically embraced while sliding down on the sofa! Oh my God, I felt I was in seventh heaven to be wrapped in this amazing man's arms! Me, who had thought so little of herself and was so wounded from the past… and him, someone who recognized the softness and beauty in me. A man whom I had finally opened up my heart and soul to and who still embraced me with love!

Lying on the sofa and feeling so much passion, all I could think of was the memory of years ago when he had made subtle suggestions and innuendoes of our possible getting together. I had just ignored them, as I was not sure what he had meant and he was married too then. It was all coming back to me now: his laughter, his smiles, tenderly helping me on with my long grey coat; how our eyes always connected with each other's, even through my shyness. It all seemed to be coming together now!

Hardly able to breathe we continued kissing when I felt his warm hand on my breast through my dress! I was ecstatic, never wanting it to end! We were lying side by side caressing one another.

My legs were moving with excitement, so he put his strong legs around mine to relax me. His kiss was so tender and gentle, not hard or rushed as some men's were.

Finally we slowly sat up while he brushed his hand over his hair, saying, "This is magical, Anne. Why didn't this happen a long time ago?" he asked.

"I did not know it was possible?" I replied.

"Of course it is. We are both adults here aren't we, Anne?"

"Yes we are, Paul," I replied contemplatively while using his first name.

His Caring

"I want you to come to my home the first time we make love, Anne, because it is very special to me!" Paul said. I eagerly agreed. He continued, "I do not have all the time in the world — I am writing a book and in a relationship, but I can spare an hour here and there. Are you okay with this?"

"Oh, yes," I responded.

"Then we can do half therapy and half loving together, if you feel you can separate the two?" he asked.

"Of course," I responded. I did not mind — I felt so honored that this doctor in La Jolla, so well respected, could want me. *I could adjust*, I thought.

Dr. Brady added: "This must remain a secret between us, Anne, as people would not understand." I agreed without hesitation that I would be silent. I was just so thrilled to be with a mature, older, intelligent man who understood so much about life and me. He also explained how difficult the world was "out there" and that this would be our special time together away from this hectic life outside. I was taking it all in and thinking he must be right, especially after all of my problems!

The First Time

It was late in the evening when I arrived at his home about a week later. Dr. Brady greeted me at the door wearing a brown bathrobe and holding a glass of white wine in his hand. His sandy-colored hair was neatly combed, and his bright blue eyes were penetrating mine with a welcoming smile on his face. I was wearing the blue dress that he liked. His friend, who was visiting, was in the next room sleeping, so we had to be quiet. Paul explained that they had been working on a book and documentary together. The man was some kind of a mystic. I was aware of this because Dr. Brady often brought it up in his office during our sessions.

We sat down on his sofa in the living room, the fireplace crackling as he began to kiss me.

"Oh, those sweet wonderful lips of yours," Paul said. His home was right on the La Jolla Shores coast. Looking around his comfortable living room, I noticed photos of his four children on the fireplace mantle. *They were so lovely*, I thought. I felt extremely special to be part of his life now. It was unfathomable that this was happening to me. I was sure we would be a family along with my two lovely children. They needed a father and I a husband like him, who also turned out to be so distinguished and well known. It seemed to be in the stars, so to speak.

Before long, Dr. Brady took my hand and led me to his bedroom. There was soft music playing and his cream-colored drapes were partially opened with a view of the ocean moonlight shining on it. A fireplace was crackling in his room as well. He gently placed me on his large king-sized bed and was soon on top of me smiling, caressing me and kissing me all over! The first time was always so special, but was extremely so with him. There seemed to be "magic in the air," as he said. Something amazingly strong connected us, more than just chemistry! We made passionate love most of the night while he whispered loving things in my ear about my beauty and sensitivity. We simply could not stop after so many years of knowing one another and having a yearning for this somewhere in the back of our minds!

It was dawn when I awakened in his arms, listening to the melody of the waves outside. The excitement, tenderness, and warmth of that evening had been more than I could have ever imagined! Little did I know the immense life-altering changes that would take place in my life and family after this lovely and meaningful evening together.

"Anne age 30."

CHAPTER 6

THERAPY AND SEX

A Silent Seduction

There was no turning back for me. I was totally enraptured by him. It seemed okay to have some therapy then sex, although this did not happen every time. But it kept me coming back. Still I felt a longing in my heart for more, as though something was left out of the whole picture of love. Then I would remember my tumultuous past experiences, so I continued to see him at his office for at least some recompense of love. It was a silent seduction of my mind!

I decided to leave my father's practice at this time and found a new job in medicine at Scripps's clinic in La Jolla. I thought It would enhance my self-esteem to work in such a renowned hospital and clinic. It was also closer to Dr. Brady's office and home, and my children could attend better schools as well. I rented a lovely home with my sister in the east side of La Jolla, which was more affordable than by the beach. This could mean a better life and independence.

One evening, Dr. Brady planned on coming over for a night of romance. I was so excited to show him my home while my children were asleep! However, when he saw my garage door open, he became nervous and left. Dr. Brady told me later that he was afraid my parents might be there. It was disheartening for me as it was hard enough having quality time together!

A few weeks later he telephoned me again in the evening and asked me if I would like to come over to his home. His voice was so warm and inviting I was so in love with him. But I had been at my grandmother's funeral that day and he thought it would be best to wait! I could feel depression setting in now. Although I was tired from the long day and loss of my wonderful grandma, I still would have gone over to see him, if only for comfort.

Acting Out

The silent seduction of therapy and sex can make a person act out the therapist's desires and wishes inside and outside of the office. One day I went to see Dr. Brady and I told him that one of my father's wealthy patients wanted to take me out. He was about twenty years older than me and married! Dr. Brady encouraged me to see him, saying, "Don't you know, Anne, that a beautiful young woman like you can really cause older men to have hard-ons? They really get excited with a younger woman. This could open a door for you to be taken care of and gain some more financial support."

"Oh, I replied, feeling a bit confused when he casually proclaimed this. Truly I hadn't thought of it that way, but I always listened — he was the professional, after all. I ended up seeing the man for a month. He was not attractive but, as I said, was a wealthy patient of my father's. He wanted to buy a house for us where he could visit. His wife was actually all right with this!

My children and I did enjoy his beautiful yacht, but I found his personality to be aggressive, while not feeling the deep connection with him that I did with Dr. Brady. My father was shocked when I told him and intervened, explaining that it was not a good situation and the man did not have my best intentions! It made me wonder what I was doing, as I knew my children and I did not fit into that lifestyle! I immediately conveyed this to him, despite his disappointment!

The Doctors I knew

I was meeting nice doctors at work now; a couple had taken a shine to me, and I flirted with them as well. It was an unconscious behavior I was unaware of at the time, but would discover later that I felt it was my "role" as a woman.

The oncologist I was employed with asked me out to lunch a couple of times. He was a silver fox, divorced, and an authentically nice person, I felt, who exuded great warmth for people. I truly enjoyed our humanitarian conversations and lunches. Although we liked one another, I somehow knew it was nothing serious.

Then there was the cardiologist in the hospital I worked with in the treadmill department. He reminded me of Paul (Dr. Brady) as he was tan, small, and very pleasant. Sometimes in the hospital hallway we made eyes at each other. One day he slightly pushed me into his nearby office, while closing the door, then placed my hand on his slacks, telling me how excited I made him! It was a surprise and flattering but I quickly left thinking that Dr. Brady was correct when he told me about older men! Our flirtations ceased soon; as he was married, we both mutually stopped.

Another time the nursing staff went out to happy hour with some of the doctors. We were all in a van when a handsome dark-haired physician began kissing me. I knew he had had a few drinks, though, and we were all just having fun! The following day one of the nurses shared with me that he had had a sexual problem and was going through a divorce. I understood then his seeming neediness!

A few months later I was delivering lab work to an internist. We struck up a conversation and later that evening I received a telephone call from him asking me to dinner. "Oh," I replied, "aren't you married?" and he quickly responded that he was separated. I agreed to dinner, but explained that it would have to be early as I had two children at home.

After dinner he stopped by his office, wanting to show me A new piece of equipment. It was dusk by now and not a soul around. He proceeded to take his new ultrasound machine to demonstrate it—by rolling it on my stomach. But when he began kissing me I pushed him away, insisting that he take me home! I was disgusted by the whole thing, feeling it was some kind of trick! This physician was also older than me and kinky, I surmised! I was so sorry that I ever went to dinner with him!

Finally, there was a retired physician from Rancho Santa Fe whom I had met with a newspaper ad. He "jumped horses and had a beautiful home in Rancho Santa Fe!" He invited me, Nadine, and Sean over to meet his children from a previous marriage. They were very young like mine and darling. I remembered bandaging the little girl after she cut her hand outside. I did enjoy seeing our children play together as well, but that didn't always make a good marriage, I thought—and the doctor could have been my grandfather! I think he enjoyed my motherly ways! And the way he discussed marriage was in a very businesslike manner. When he contacted me again at New Year's to invite me to "the Gala Party at the Ranch," I boldly told him that I had made plans to go out with a girlfriend! He was very insulted at this and I was glad, because I hated the way he treated his cook—so subordinately—and was beginning to do the same with me!

That was it, I thought! I ran back to Dr. Brady telling him that I just could not do this anymore! It was not for me! Couldn't anyone see the good in me and my children and appreciate it besides Dr. Brady? I began to wonder why I had to go "hunting" for someone to take care of us, when Dr. Brady was right there, seeming to think that I was so wonderful?

CHAPTER 7

Our Own World

Anticipation

After telling Dr. Brady that I quit dating, he wrapped me in his arms, saying, "Oh, Anne, I would love to take you home and marry you!" He understood my challenges and loved me anyway! His words of marriage made me so happy then, and I cherished them while hanging onto this dream! I began to upgrade my cooking skills to prepare for this day and stayed in the best shape possible.

Medications

I continued to take the medicines prescribed by Dr. Brady. There was no other recourse. If I didn't, I experienced tearfulness along with past unhappy memories as though reliving them! No doubt I needed them, I presumed, as he was the expert! Although I was still spacey on the medicines, I could at least make it through the day. And Paul had told me, "Think of it like taking your vitamins."

A Symbiotic Relationship

"At this juncture in "therapy," our relationship had become what is known as "symbiotic," (a word I learned later). I could not live without him, and he was attached to me as well. He had become my lifeline now. Of course I loved my beautiful children, but I also longed for a mate to complete myself and family! It was only natural and I had waited a long time!

While mentioning my mother on one of my visits, I thought it nice he acknowledged that, "she meant well," even if she was set in her ways! Then he added, "Anne, you are just the opposite kind of woman. You have feminine aspects, which I adore."

Dr. Brady was deeply concerned about how much I had on my shoulders in life. He really would like to help me out was his constant reassurance. He filled out a medical form requesting disability for me. But mostly we shared this special unique time together for love, "away from the crazy world out there" as he would put it. I cherished our exclusive times together. Never had I been this intimate with a man before, so trusting and accepting, and true to one's heart!

Once we had a "picnic" in his office when I was the last appointment of the day. I packed a little wine and two gourmet dinners from The French Gourmet in La Jolla. It was fun and romantic evening together!

Another time I "looked so pretty," he said, "in my purple pantsuit," that he rushed home to get his protection for our rendezvous, while I waited in his private office!

Christmas time of 1987 I gave him a Fisherman's Irish sweater. He called to thank me, telling me it was the nicest knit sweater he had ever received. And then I sent him a dozen red roses, signing it, "from a secret admirer." After all, he had stopped charging me for my office visits, and I was grateful.

My Children

Dr. Brady expressed his desire to help me by seeing my children for some quality time with them. I eagerly agreed to this so that they could become acquainted with him for the future! *This is especially kind of him to help me out with my children as well,* I told myself.

Nadine walked over to his office on her lunch hour from school for a few visits with him. I encouraged this, feeling that it would be nice for them to become acquainted too. He played chess with her and chatted. She was going through puberty and having some moodiness, and he thought it would be a good idea for her to take the same antidepressant that I was on. However, Nadine relayed to me that it made her very tired in school! She was eleven years old and wise enough to throw the pills out, while not telling this to Dr. Brady! In fact, we decided she had enough visits after that.

Sean only saw him a couple of times. He was particularly shy at about six years old. I know my children were having some trouble adjusting to our move to La Jolla and their new school. Anyway, Sean still had a "Big Brother" from the association, whom he related to very well. Then another change was about to occur in our lives.

My grandmother, who passed away, left her home for us to live in. As it had become too expensive to stay in La Jolla, I chose the more practical way and moved back to Oceanside, beside Carlsbad. The children were delighted, of course, to be back with their friends, familiar school, and extended family!

I was quite unhappy leaving the area of Dr. Brady, but knew it was best for now. Paul also thought it the practical thing to do, but underneath it all I was wondering about *our relationship!*

CHAPTER 8

TRANSFERENCE

Trusted

The building of trust with a doctor begins with his title of authority. It expands with his years of expertise and practice. Then of course his age, along with the wisdom it confers, is also very beneficial. There is also the background of family, friends, and other professionals who hold him in high regard.

Then there is the consistency of appointments, discussions and advice which deepen this intimate trust and bond, until one feels safe enough to reveal their innermost issues, needs, and the desires of their hearts and souls! Along with the doctors' Hippocratic Oath and high ethical standards, all of these create a sacred trust and bond! At times this intimacy can become closer than a marriage, especially one that may be lacking in any way.

There, in the confines of his office, I formed a very trusting relationship with Dr. Brady. It is in the hands of the physician that we entrust our minds, souls, and lives, with! The doctor holds authority and power over his patients who are vulnerable due to suffering, illness, or loss!

I knew with Dr. Brady's reputable background that I could depend on him for the help and wisdom that I needed then. Being well renowned and a family's psychiatrist made it easy to trust him! Straightening out my life was imperative to me, and I was grateful to be receiving his expert advice while depending on him.

Over many years we had become emotionally close. This was a safe haven for me to unfold who I was, where I came from, and how to see life in a better light, while learning from an expert mentor and teacher. As a divorced young single mother I felt, at the time, that I had no one else to turn to.

In matters of the heart, I was not emotionally close to my parents. This created an avenue of trust with Dr. Brady as well. He was another parent figure for me, although I did not understand this at the time. Nor was I aware of something called "transference"! He had been the only psychiatrist I had ever seen. Under these delicate circumstances in psychotherapy, transference occurs. As the patient draws closer to a therapist, needs and unhealed wounds in one's life are transferred unconsciously over to the psychiatrist or psychologist.

Often, issues are from childhood or other important relationships. Transference is supposed to happen in order for the therapist to address the needs of the patient in a professional and ethical manner! This opens up a doorway for healing and self-discovery to move forward for the patient, creating a healthier happier life. Transference is the core of therapy.

"Transference" is defined in the *Merriam Webster Dictionary* as: "The redirection of feelings and desires and especially of those unconsciously retained from childhood toward a new object (as a psychoanalyst conducting therapy)."

The *Wikipedia Dictionary* has words relating to the context of therapy: "Transference is often manifested as an erotic attraction towards a therapist, but can be seen in many forms such as rage, mistrust, parentification, extreme dependence, or even placing the therapist in a god-like … status."

Then there is "counter transference," which is defined as redirection of a therapist's feeling toward a patient, or more generally, as a therapist's emotional entanglement with a patient."

Subtle Longing

About three years after becoming sexually involved with Dr. Brady and while having dinner with my parents and family, I quietly asked my father if we could have Dr. Brady over one evening for dinner. It would be especially nice, I presumed, for him to become more sociable with my family.

Looking surprised, my father replied, "Well, you know Anne, you have to be careful: there is something called *transference* which happens with a therapist, so it would not be a good idea to have him to dinner." Not sure what he really meant, I felt left out again of my own desires. Seeing my dismay, Dad added, with a smile, "It is easy for patients to fall in love with their doctors!"

But I knew this was different. I knew that my feelings for Paul were real love and that he felt the same way! I guess I wanted it to be in the open. However I said nothing more, remembering that Dr. Brady had requested our relationship to stay private. Still, I continued to hope that someday soon it would change!

I could not help my subtle longing to be with him; it seemed so natural. It seemed to overshadow everything else in my life. I went to work, took care of my children, but he was always in the back of my mind, as if driven by some unconscious force. Generally we would meet at his office to discuss my issues around family, money, or my career. At times, after thirty minutes of therapy, we would make quiet love on the carpet or sofa. Sometimes he would cover my mouth, to remind me there were people in the outer rooms. A few times I did meet him at his home, at night, which I always loved, but mostly it was in the office. One time he had a meeting with his medical group and asked me to page him so he could leave the meeting to see me. I did this and was so flattered that he would think of our needs over the medical meeting!

At the end of the day, having the last appointment was especially meaningful to me, as I knew that it was "our time alone," as he had expressed. I remembered wearing my pretty dark polka-dot stockings one night with my blue knit dress! We were lying down on the office sofa and I raised one of my legs up, showing off my stockings while we laughed, and he asked me, "Are you sure you don't have the measles?" I felt so free and had so much fun being myself, and I felt secure in his embrace. Not having to put on any airs, I was finally relieved to be myself.

Entrapment

Time was slipping away, however, and I made no real personal growth or progress regarding my own needs and situation. All this time, I just assumed we would marry. Paul also said to me one day that he wished we had adjoining homes and he could just see me whenever we wanted. "Wouldn't that be perfect?" he happily stated.

I knew one day his book and documentary would be finished, and then we could be married. I would wait for him. Meanwhile, he was still trying to claim disability for me so that I could stay home with my children. He understood how "difficult it was for a woman to raise a family and have a career, too. It just wasn't fair in today's society." I agreed that my main focus was being a mother, and someday a good wife. I felt so close to him in our own world, with no one outside to bother us! I continued on my medications to remain stable. Although I felt somewhat anxious about the future, my only recourse was to stay bonded to him for hope.

CHAPTER 9

THE SPRING OF '88

Marry me when...

The years were slipping away and I began wondering if Dr. Brady was actually contemplating marriage. I knew the project he often spoke of in the office was very important to him, but it was approaching eight years now since our intimate relationship began when I was thirty—and I had first met him when I was nineteen! The dreams for me and my children seem to be fading.

I couldn't help but tell my father, this time, that Dr. Brady had expressed to me one day that he wished he could take me home and marry me. As though relieved, Dad replied, "Well, I wish he would, too!" It had been seven years since I had been seeing him as a patient consistently now! Dad had no idea that we were sexually involved, and I knew he just wanted me to have a better life! It made me feel very happy that Dad had said that, of course—I was sure he would be proud if I married a doctor, too.

Years earlier, I had confided to Nadine of my involvement with Dr. Brady, insisting that she keep the secret. It was not a good thing to do to a child, but I wasn't aware at the time. Now, though, she was almost seventeen and Sean thirteen! It surely seemed time to have a discussion with Paul regarding our relationship — in fact, way overdue I reflected.

However, when I attempted to see Dr. Brady he sounded rather frustrated, saying that he was going through depositions and very busy with them. He proceeded to explain that he had been falsely accused of being involved with a female patient. My heart went out to him, knowing that it was not true and he certainly did not deserve this! His trust was indisputable to me, as we had a special bond. I was not aware of the term "depositions," so he attempted to explain it to me.

Now that he was so engrossed with this accusation and attorneys, it would be few months before we could meet. As the holidays were nearing, I could focus more on my children and extended family, I thought, which was always a happy time! There would be shopping, decorating, wonderful family meals, and just having fun together! And before I knew it, Easter was around the corner and I was able to finally see Dr. Brady!

My Last Appointment

It was April 10th, the spring of 1988, and everything was in bloom on my way to his office. My favorite time of year had arrived, and something was in the air I could feel it. Perhaps it would finally be time for us to become true partners, and his project would be published as well! Now I would have a heart-to-heart conversation with him. Little did I know that this would be my last visit!

My appointment was at the usual time, in the evening. It was a balmy night as we snuggled on the sofa, the wind gently swaying the lavender Wisteria vine and palm trees outside his office window. Seagulls were soaring above us against a pink and blue sunset sky! As we smothered each other with kisses while caressing one another, it became obvious that we truly needed this time together.

Paul's heart was beating next to mine, but as I began to unbutton his shirt, he surprisingly became hesitant, saying, "I have to be careful, Anne. The depositions are making me edgy."

With this, I decided that it would not be the best time to discuss our relationship. Instead, I intuitively supported him, expressing empathy for him.

After several endearing moments, he suddenly began slipping his hand under my pleated floral skirt, unable to hold himself back anymore! We were soon immersed in one another down on the sofa, he on top of me. The warmth of the evening and there being no one around, not even the staff, made it especially passionate! As he pulled my lace blouse up, my breasts overflowed onto his now bare chest! Heat from our bodies exuded all around us as we excitedly exploded together!

Leaving his office while gazing upward, I admired a beautiful array of stars sparkling in the dark evening sky. We had been together for two wonderful hours! and I was now carrying his baby!

Expecting

It was just two weeks later after my visit with Paul that I suspected I might be pregnant. I always knew the signs: tender breast sensations, waking up in the middle of the night to use the bathroom, and having cramps in my legs.

Even early on like this I could tell! I was in awe and happy and amazed all at the same time. But I had to wait two more weeks for a test to be accurate before giving him the news. And indeed it was positive.

My excitement could not be contained: I had to open up to Nadine one night while taking a bath. She was surprised as well and happy for me too, while hoping Dr. Brady would be. I decided to wait awhile to share the news, so that I could just immerse myself with this precious life within me!

One evening in bed, *while stroking my abdomen, I sensed a telepathic communication with my baby, saying, "Children of the light are being born to assist mankind to a higher consciousness!"* I was so touched and knew that this was possible. My grandmother had a gift of seeing visions from a higher source. Still, it was natural between a mother and baby if they were really in tune with one another, and especially in a meditative state and with soft music on.

Upon turning seven weeks, I thought it was time give Paul the news. When I phoned him at home one evening, he said that he was in a rush, having to go to a meeting and we would have to talk later. As he seemed preoccupied again, I decided to write a letter to him about the pregnancy.

Confrontation

In the letter I expressed my love for him and that we were expecting a baby. I was thrilled and happy about this, and as it had been many years for both of us, this would be a wonderful time in our lives to share our special beautiful baby. Of course, I added that I loved him very much!

Two days after I mailed the letter, I received a phone call from him late that night. His first question to me was, "Are you sure it is mine?"

"Of course, I have not been with anyone else!" I responded shockingly! He then apologized for being abrupt with me on the phone the other night and that, if he had known why I was calling, he would not have done that.

Paul wanted to come over right away, but I explained that it was too late for me and the children were in bed. He was insistent on seeing me the next day, though, and did not want my children there! Dr. Brady was beginning to sound rather anxious, which also made me nervous.

The following day I sent my children to friends for a couple of hours as he drove over. Entering my home he looked around, saying that it was quite nice. I realized that this was the first time he had been there, which seemed rather odd. He took my hand, saying, "Let's go over to the sofa—like we do in my office, Anne." I thought that a bit strange as well, but proceeded to follow him there.

As we sat down on my sofa, he put his arm around my shoulders while asking me to tell him what happened. I explained, "I was on birth control but had missed a few days." I was afraid to tell him that I had actually tossed out my pills, as I had not seen him in so long. I continued, saying, "Our last lovemaking was very intense. That is all I know and now I am pregnant!"

Paul's response was, "We cannot have this baby, Anne. I am in trouble already and it will ruin my career!"

I replied, "No one has to know, and I would take good care of our baby. I am already in love with the baby and I love carrying your baby, too—and I will not have an abortion!" I had thought he would be pleased, that it would make him proud of me and love me even more! I also told him that "the stars do it!"

He retorted back, "We aren't the stars, Anne!"

That hurt, and I told him, "I thought you loved me, Paul!"

He sighed heavily and said: "I do love you Anne—as a patient—but not this way!" adding, "You need intellectual pursuits!"

He had never mentioned this before and hearing it made me feel more upset after all the years of being with him! When he asked me if anyone else knew about this, I hesitated but told him, "Yes—my daughter knows!"

Dr. Brady threw his head back in frustration, saying, "How could you do that, Anne. She will tell others."

I responded that Nadine would not tell: that it was our secret, too.

Then while putting his hands on his head in anger, he asked if I would see a friend of his who was a nurse. She could explain some things to me as a woman. I agreed that I would see her, but I really was not sure. As he rose from the sofa heading towards the door, he said meanly: "Anne, I do *not* want to be the father of your baby, and I want nothing do with your family at all!"

It felt as if a dagger suddenly pierced my heart, and I began to feel faint and dizzy as I knew he meant my mother, father, brothers and sisters, as well as my children and our baby. He continued very strongly, telling me, "I will commit suicide if you go through with this, Anne!" Now with his voice rising, almost yelling, he said, "I have a mean streak in me and I will use it if needed!" Dr. Brady then slammed the door behind him!

After this I became very shaky and frightened! I had never seen him angry and he had never been mean to me! My breathing became very rapid and I lay down on my sofa weeping uncontrollably. *Oh God, what had happened!* My sweet children returned momentarily, coming right over to comfort me. They put their loving arms around me trying to console me. Sean did not know anything about the pregnancy, as he was young. Nadine was so wise, telling me that I should do what I want. I said that I would and that I loved them both very much! But my life was about to change drastically!

CHAPTER 10

SECRETS AND LIES

The Nurse

The following morning I received a phone call from Dr. Brady's friend Sue, the nurse. After introducing herself, she inquired of a convenient time to meet. Since she sounded nice, I agreed to see her the next evening, only because it was Dr. Brady's desire. Sue was employed at the Neonatal Care with Children's hospital in San Diego.

She was probably about twenty years older than me, as her hair was white. Offering her some coffee, we sat at my green breakfast table. She was congenial while attempting to become a little acquainted with me. The nurse knew about my involvement with Dr. Brady, telling me that he had discussed it with her. "People can make mistakes, Anne," she said. I wondered what she meant by that, but did not respond.

Continuing, she then asked me, "What would you do with another child, as you seem to have your hands full already?"

I proclaimed, "I loved being a mother and it was not a problem. I have also known Paul for twenty years now."

Although she seemed surprised at the revelation, she continued her questioning, wondering how I could support three children and work.

"I am perfectly capable," I answered. I did not want to discuss my personal relationship with Paul nor my hopes. Sue went on to inform me that the medicines I was taking could harm the fetus. I jumped in to let her know that I had discontinued them two weeks into my pregnancy, I was not worried and would "let nature take its course!"

Being persistent, she informed me, "Dr. Brady is burning the candle at both ends!" and, "He is "just beside himself, a very busy doctor, very reputable, and that this could ruin him!" I did not comprehend this at all as I felt he was very stable and could handle anything, although I did not say that to her either!

However, I was beginning to feel guilty then, as though I had done something wrong and felt sorry for him as well! Still, I emphatically explained to her that I was overjoyed and had no plans to have an abortion. She encouraged me to think about it and what I was doing, stating, "I just wouldn't know what to do with a baby at your age of thirty-eight!" Slowly she began to bring up abortion for these reasons, and that I could have one out of town and she would be happy to find a clinic for me. She concluded by saying that I should definitely make up my mind soon, as I was already nine weeks pregnant!

Still trying to be congenial, I agreed that I would think about things. Feeling very pressured and nervous at this point and wanting her to leave, I began walking toward the door so she would realize this. Before walking out, Sue assured me that if I had any questions I could call her, otherwise she would check in with me later in the week. I nodded my head and closed the door firmly behind her.

Father Mike

After much contemplation, I felt the need to speak with someone objective. I suddenly remembered Father Mike, an independent priest who was extremely down to earth. He had been friends with my father for forty years and I truly admired his work with the poor. Often he would bring them to my dad's office for treatment and he would never charge them.

He was kind enough to see me the following day at his home in Encinitas. After explaining my predicament, Father Mike, with his warm and concerned eyes, said, "You have been taken advantage of and used! This doctor, if he were any kind of a man, should marry you, Anne, and take responsibility for his actions!" *I'm the one who somehow feels guilty now though,* I thought!

Father Mike added that he himself as a man had been sitting down with a pretty young women. He had temptations in his life but had never acted on them, because of regard for his position and for ethics and morals, which always reminded him never to cross those boundaries. I was a little taken aback from this, as I had never thought of him that way: even though he was quite a handsome man, he was always a priest first to me.

"Making you have an abortion, Anne, is outright wrong!" he said, and continuing he offered to call this doctor and talk to him! I explained that it had all been a secret and I just wasn't ready for that. "Well, Anne," he said, "the Holy Spirit will take care of you." I really did not understand about the Holy Spirit taking care of me—I did not see how. I had not practiced my faith in years, suddenly recalling the times I would go to the Self-Realization Temple in Encinitas with my children. Father Mike then took my hands while saying prayers for me with a blessing. He hugged me goodbye, telling me to keep him informed. I did feel somehow relieved in his presence, I thought as I left.

His Rage My Terror

The following afternoon, Dr. Brady called to see how I was feeling. I told him I was very tired. He said, "Yes, my first wife was tired in the afternoons due to hormonal changes brought on by pregnancy." Then, in a stronger voice, he asked me what I had decided. "I am still thinking things over, but I do not want another abortion," I told him.

Sounding frantic then, he offered me money, saying, "We would see each other socially now if you would just get the abortion!" He emphasized that he had too much to lose and that we could not go on this way anymore in secret. I wondered, *Why now?* Deep down I could feel myself getting angry at his attitude. I did not want to give him a quick or easy answer. Upset, he continued, while again raising his voice, "There isn't much time to think about things!" and repeated his threat, "I will commit suicide if you go through with this pregnancy, Anne!" As we hung up the phone I could not stop shaking! I was terrified of the circumstances and him too! I feared he might really kill himself and that it would be my fault! I felt so all alone. He had been my stabilizing force, my life, my love. Now it was all drastically changing and shattering.

I would fall asleep at night with my hands on my abdomen, comforting the baby and playing soft music while feeling so connected already to this soul. There was a spiritual bond and essence between us with immense love! And now I was trapped not knowing what to do! Everything Father Mike had said to me I didn't hear anymore!

Against My Will

A day later the nurse called to let me know that she knew of a place in Santa Monica where I could go and no one would know. Paul would give me the money for the abortion. I was caving in and said I would look into it. But I really did not want to, nor did I.

Having told my brother Eric that I was pregnant but the father was not happy, he and his wife offered to adopt the baby even though they had four children of their own. It was so kind and beautiful of them, but I truly knew, though, that I could not give my baby up. I thanked them, telling them that I would keep in touch to let them know what I would decide. I had not told my brother that it was Dr. Brady's baby at the time.

Suddenly I was ten weeks pregnant. With all of the pressure from Dr. Brady and Sue, I now felt scared to death! I felt threatened that I was ruining his career and even his life, especially after he said that he would commit suicide.

I called Paul, wanting to come over to see him at his home and talk. He refused, saying there was no purpose in it and that he would only see me again socially after everything was "taken care of." The next morning I brought my children over to my parents' home and drove frantically to the San Diego clinic to have the abortion.

The clinic wanted to know if I had an abortion before and when I said yes, they responded that

I knew what it was about then. Half in a trance I followed their direction without thinking. It was over fast and I pretended that I was okay. In truth I was not. I was numb, but I knew Paul and I would at least see each other now, he being the love of my life. That was all that really mattered, I surmised. I cared for him and did what he wanted. He had helped me for so many years and even stopped charging me for my office visits. I had no right to put this pressure on him.

The Hotel

In a daze I drove myself to the hotel in La Jolla where we planned on meeting. I arrived around 5:00 PM; Dr. Brady was supposed to be there soon, but four hours had gone by. Meanwhile I was bleeding and feeling ill to my stomach, while dizziness and cramps were setting in. I was on the eighth floor of the hotel room where the balcony overlooked La Jolla, the beautiful view that I so loved!

After five hours of waiting, my mind began to wonder as I pondered the possibility of dying! I did not have any conscious plans of anything, still I slowly began walking toward the balcony, imagining myself falling from it!

At that moment a *cloud surrounded me, stopping me from going further.* It was an angelic presence: *and a* voice said to me: "You will become a powerful woman, and you will sue Dr. Brady.

You still have a journey ahead of you." I raised my arms as if trying to stop this force around me while answering, "No! I love him and would never sue him!" Then the spiritual presence left. A moment later there was a knock at the door; it was Paul Brady — it was now 10:00 PM.

He was over four hours late, but I ignored it. He never even sat down. As I wanted to be comforted I went towards him, but he pulled away from me, saying, "No, I only came to see if everything went all right." I confirmed yes it did. Then he told me he could not see me again, not socially or as a patient either!

I begged him to stay with me. I did not understand this side of him or why he would act like this. He promised that after the abortion, he would see me and continue our relationship outside of his office! Now he turned around quickly going through the hotel door, not even looking back, leaving me abandoned and alone. I went to the bed trembling, lying down sinking into a deep void, not knowing what to do with my life now or how to face my children, nor what I had done!

I truly felt my only recourse was suicide. I had so many failures, but in the past my children kept me going. I could never do anything to harm them or leave them. However, I thought they were older now and I just did not think I could survive this! One more blow — how could I even get up anymore? My heart ached so much and I did not know who I was anymore!

After all the years I had known Dr. Brady — since I was nineteen years old — I just could not get it out of my mind! Where did I go wrong? What had happened? He was my doctor and my lover, and I thought that he loved me! Now he has totally abandoned me! I did what he asked against my own will. How could he just leave me this way? It was ominous! I just felt my spirit slipping into a void of nothingness!

I phoned my closest friend for support and when I told her what had happened, her response was that I had made my decision, so I should get on with life and that we were both adults! I hung up the phone while sinking into remorse.

I just lay there for hours praying for God to help me. I didn't want to go on anymore. I could not get up. I felt my life had just crumbled around me. My love, my baby, my dreams and future — all vanished in an instant. It seemed like déjà vu! I lay there in shock all through the night, unable to move or even cry!

"Broken, Abandoned, Alone."

CHAPTER 11

REPRESSION

I come to you naked and abandoned today, Lord,

I ask for your loving guidance and hand to help

Me through this crisis. My baby has gone to heaven,

I am left here alone, weeping with my broken heart.

Shock

E arly the next morning I slowly arose from the hotel bed weak and dazed, then carefully stepped into the shower while grasping the bars. The warm water gently caressed my aching body, which felt so wounded now! As blood flowed from my womb, a gush of tears poured down my face falling onto my breasts, still filled with milk! I slumped down to the tile floor, letting the water wash over me. I just sat there in a puddle of lavender soap weeping, feeling so naked and alone!

Forty minutes passed before I managed to pull myself up, then combed my sopping hair. Shivering now, I wrapped myself up in the soft blue blanket on the bed, remaining for another hour. I was still alive in some way, at least I was aware of this. My children would be waiting for me to pick them up at my parents' home, so I slipped my summer dress on, the one Paul had once loved, and quietly left the hotel in the morning mist.

On the way home I pulled into Torrey Pines Beach, feeling a need to rest and breathe in the fresh air. No one was around this early in the morning. I lay down on nature's bed of brown leaves for some time, as I did not want my family to see me upset and broken. I prayed again for help, then continued my journey home.

My parents did not know what had happened, just that I was very tired. They assumed I had been at my girlfriends that night. I was not about to tell them, being the faithful Catholics that they were.

As soon as we arrived home I fell in bed, just needing to sleep! Nadine came in to check on me to see if I was all right. I smiled at her loving face with her beautiful green eyes and light brown hair, replying, "Yes, I am." I could only pretend, of course, for their sake. But she saw that I was weak and overwrought!

Nightmares and Flashbacks

I awakened in the middle of the night with hideous nightmares about the abortion. I saw my baby being lifted up to heaven then falling from the sky. Another nightmare was that I was nursing her, whom I so loved, and she was crying out to me. This began happening every night, and I would perspire awakening with my heart pounding and having difficulty breathing.

Then came nightmares of Dr. Brady looking for me with a gun and raping me over and over. Some would be of running away trying to hide in a war zone, while feeling very terrified of being found! I was not sure what all of this meant, but I felt somehow trapped in a room in my mind. Sean came in to see how I was too. He would sit on my bed for a while, staring at me with his deep blue eyes of concern. I patted his blonde hair, bringing back fond memories of him as a baby. I had breastfed him for two-and-a-half years. It was a beautiful time in my life of bonding with my children. They were still so young and innocent, I reminisced, and so concerned about me. I was their only parent, but now it felt that I was the child and they the parents!

My issues were not better but in fact increased. I now was having some flashbacks about the abortion and that it really happened! I would see a little baby girl in a stroller by my house or at the children's school and it would trigger these memories, along with unbearable grief over everything that had occurred! I would have to discontinue what I was doing in order to catch my breath and bring myself into the present.

I could not socialize at all other than with my family. I rarely spoke to anyone! Nadine could obviously see how disturbed I was that I had had the abortion! She so wished that I had not listened to Dr. Brady, who hurt me so horrendously!

The Internist

Sue, the nurse, called to see if I wanted to meet with her. I told her that I would have to wait as I was not up to it now. A week later I agreed to see her at a restaurant in La Jolla. While eating a salad and having a couple of glasses of Chardonnay, she attempted to be compassionate, saying that it was the best for everyone. *But "they" were not me,* I thought! Now I had no desire to open up to her, as I did not trust her anymore! The encounter with Sue made me realize that I needed professional help, but not hers!

As I felt so mentally scattered and with little resources, I first went to a free clinic and saw a female internist. She was extremely comforting and empathetic. After describing the effects of the abortion and how I felt forced to have it, I now I feared that I might commit suicide. I did not open up to her about the father! She was very concerned, asking me if I had thought of how I would do it. I explained that if I did, I saw myself drifting out to sea forever and ever, just vanishing into the depths of the ocean. And that it seemed the perfect and easy way to leave!

The internist encouraged me to return for help. She gave me a phone number to call if I felt like I was in any danger. But I never went back. I was too embarrassed and scared. On top of that I was beginning to dissociate.

I phoned Dr. Brady at his home, conveying to him the difficulty I was having. He immediately retorted, "You are not my patient anymore, Anne, so I will refer you to another doctor. I will mail a letter of referral to him, telling him that you had romanticized over me and that I felt it better for you to see someone else." Then he added that, "You just can't tell him that we were involved."

"Of course not," I replied, adding, "I had no intention of mentioning us."

CHAPTER 12

To Trust Again

A "Real" Therapist

I t was June 28th, the fifth day after the abortion, when I met Dr. Ansel. I had just about begged him to see me, asking if he would take Medi-Cal and explaining that I would have private insurance within a month. Although he hesitated with this piece of information, he did agree to see me once for an evaluation, and then he would decide whether he would take me on as a patient.

Dr. Ansel's office was on the other side of La Jolla, by Pacific Beach. It was easy to find, a simple office in a small quiet complex, which I was grateful for. When he opened the door for me I was startled and jumped with fear! He apologized for scaring me. As we walked down the hallway, I could not help but ask him sarcastically, "What kind of games do you play here?"

He frowned behind his golden beard at the question, and did not reply. I wondered if he were trustworthy.

His personal counseling office was quaint, with several relics from different countries on a large wooden bookcase. He must be a traveler and collector. He had a sturdy frame. He sat behind his desk in a black chair with a friendly smile. As soon as I sat down, I became very thirsty and nervous, asking for a glass of water. Dr. Ansel looked surprised at this, but did ask his receptionist to bring one for me. As well, my breathing was becoming rapid.

"How do you do, Anne?" he said, and added, "It's nice to meet you," and reached over to shake my hand.

Out of nowhere I blurted out that I had an abortion five days earlier and that it was a friend of my family's, a lawyer, who was the father and had coerced me into the abortion. This was my story to cover up Dr. Brady's name.

Dr. Ansel appeared inquisitive now. I explained to him that the lawyer had to keep his status, that it would look bad for him in the community and with my family if I were found pregnant by him.

The psychiatrist's mouth had a bit of a smirk on it as he said, "I am sorry that this happened to you," then proceeded to ask me, "What about you, Anne, what are your dreams and wishes?"

Upon telling him that I was a mother of two beautiful children, I broke down crying as I gulped more water. He tried to console me, saying it was okay and that I could take my time. He also wanted me to go over some of my family history and my own past. He said that he had received Dr. Brady's referral letter but would need more information.

I was reticent about repeating my background again and told him so. He replied: "This is the only way that we can make counseling work between us, Anne."

I agreed and began to describe some of my family's history to him. I explained a couple of issues and challenges along with eating disorders and depression, but opted to highlight all the wonderful gatherings and happiness we all had together in a very large Catholic family.

Again he looked a bit puzzled and responded: "Who wears the pants in this family and likes to clip the wings of the children?"

I replied, "Oh, well, I suppose my mother."

With that, Dr. Ansel stopped his writing, closing my chart. He shook his head, saying that he would like to work with me expecting regular payments after a month, with a commitment of consistent visits.

Dr. Ansel stated, "This is a codependent family with some serious issues, and the lawyer has a hold on you as well, Anne. We will have to go over this relationship." He also surmised that I was taking too much medication and instructed me to wean down from the tranquilizer, Stelazine, explaining that he would prefer regular sessions instead of just taking such a strong tranquilizer!

Again I became skeptical and sarcastic with him, stating, "Oh, so you think I need therapy?"

"I have no doubt that you need therapy, Anne," Dr. Ansel replied, closing the file and making direct eye contact with me. I decided to remain with him, realizing it was a matter of life or death now! I did not know what else to do and he appeared to be just a little older than me, which was somehow comforting.

Dr. Ansel's methodology was more straight forward than Dr. Brady's had been. I asked him to please not make me dependent on him, because I needed to be strong! No doubt he was this way anyway, expecting the patient to grow and discover their own potential.

After a few more visits he was wondering why I seemed stuck and not following through on some of my desires. Dr. Ansel spoke of *codependency,* a word I was not familiar with at the time. He referred a couple of books to me to read: *Codependent No More,* and another one on self-esteem. I was beginning to feel more comfortable with him now!

Over the next four months Dr. Ansel tried to encourage me to discuss the "lawyer" and abortion and how it had affected me. He also explained to me that I had rights and that it was wrong how I had been manipulated. As well, he was puzzled as to why I had remained in unhealthy relationships and why I wasn't advancing in my own career. A job with my father was not really being independendt, he claimed.

Truth

In autumn I telephoned Dr. Brady, asking to meet for lunch, as I still had a deep yearning to see him. He agreed to meet me at The Torrey Pines Country Club in La Jolla. After hiking 20 minutes up the beautiful path with hundreds of pine trees hovering around us, we sat on a park bench overlooking the Sea and hugged one another. Kissing me he said, "Oh, there are those wonderful lips." It was a nice moment but something seemed lacking to me. He brought up the woman who was suing him and how difficult it was. Again I consoled him, agreeing that it was a terrible thing that she was doing.

Later, while having lunch at the country club, Dr. Brady began questioning me about Dr. Ansel, mentioning that he was a different type of psychiatrist: more clear-cut and factual. Dr. Brady was also curious what we had been discussing in counseling. I imparted that it was mainly regarding my femininity and family. He wanted to be sure that his name and the fact we had been involved was not spoken of. I assured him, of course, that it was not.

To my shock, Dr. Brady disclosed to me that he had contemplated having our baby at midlife, but felt overwhelmed thinking about college money and the other necessities in life! Underneath my façade I was still extremely broken over the abortion, and hearing this unbelievable fact tore at my soul now! I could say nothing then—it hurt too much! I picked up my purse and left!

Early in September, Eric approached me in confidence at our father's office. He asked me if I had read the newspaper that morning regarding a woman who was suing Dr. Brady for sexual misconduct in his office. I said no and that Dr. Brady had explained the situation to me and that she was lying. I knew him better than that. I had finally told Eric, a few weeks earlier, that it was Dr. Brady's baby. He still thought that I should see a lawyer because it wasn't right what had happened to me, but I refused.

A couple of days later I received another phone call from Dr. Brady that would further break my heart and derail me. It was all that I could do those last few months to keep my sanity. He phoned me one night to say that there was something he needed to tell me. Then he continued to explain, "Anne, I have been sexually involved with other patients. It is going to be in the news the next day and on TV." Then, as if crying on my shoulder, he went on to express how awful his marriage had been. That he had been married for twenty years and how cold she was to him that he used to go to bed crying. As well, he hoped that I would understand.

I naturally attempted to console him once again, but deep in my heart all I could think of was my baby — how he forced me to have an abortion with his mean and threatening persistence, and claiming that he would "commit suicide" while saying he had never done anything like that before with any patients. I was fighting back tears of anger with knots in my stomach!

I could not help but say to him, "You don't practice what you preach, do you?"

He responded, "Do you know anyone who does?"

My father quickly came to my mind — I knew he did! He was an honest loving man, doctor, father and husband. As well, several of his close colleagues were, too. But I did not respond! Then I asked him, "Why didn't you take me through my childhood?"

He replied, "I didn't think you could handle it, Anne."

Feeling extremely dismayed, I told him that I had to go. He had wanted to give me some money, but I could not think about anything else except my children and life, and how terribly this had affected us for so many years. I hung up the phone.

The following morning I phoned Dr. Ansel from my father's office during lunch hour. I asked him, "What would happen to a doctor if I knew something about a patient and doctor that was not proper?"

"Well, that depends on what it is, Anne," Dr. Ansel replied, and he continued, "What exactly is it?" he asked. I carefully told him that I could not say.

He then nicely and firmly said: "Anne, if you know something that happened to a patient, it needs to be addressed so that it will not happen to someone else."

I responded, "Okay—well, let me think about it, Dr. Ansel.

A week later I had an appointment with Dr. Ansel At Mira Mesa Hospital. It was at 5:00 PM, as we were now meeting at his office in the hospital after his rounds. But after speaking with him on the phone, I suddenly became frightened and cancelled my appointment. I decided to attend a seminar on healing in San Diego instead! This was more important to me, I thought.

To my surprise, about 4:00 PM I received a telephone call from Dr. Ansel. My face became flushed and I started to perspire at the same time upon hearing his voice! He asked me why I had cancelled my appointment. I nervously explained that I had decided to attend a seminar. He replied, "Those are good for you, Anne," but since it was in San Diego, he could meet me at six at the hospital.

I stammered that I did not know how to get there from the San Diego harbor where I would be, but he calmly said that was all right—he would give me the directions. I slowly and quietly responded "Okay," despite being still unsure about it all. But feeling obligated to the therapeutic commitment I made with him, I decided to go.

When I arrived at his hospital office, I was smiling but very tense too. Nervously I began to discuss the seminar: what I learned and the healing groups. I also informed him I left the seminar early for my appointment with him.

Dr. Ansel, in his professional insightful way, asked me what was on my mind. I continued to divert to other subjects, becoming a bit confused, until he suddenly asked, "Anne, how long are you going to be on this roller coaster?" continuing with, "According to Dr. Brady's notes, it's been eight years already!"

With that remark, I harshly responded, "Well, maybe he wasn't such a good therapist!"

"Well, maybe he wasn't—still...."

I stopped him while suddenly saying emphatically, "I have been having an affair with my therapist—it was not an attorney!"

Dr. Ansel—who had been leaning back in his chair with his arms behind his head—stopped speaking. His brown eyes widened, and he slowly brought his chair down. I began shaking, crying, and laughing for the next 15 minutes. All this time Dr. Ansel sat quietly, watching me with a concerned and angry expression on his face. It was such a relief, after all of those years, to finally be able to tell someone the truth about my secret relationship with Dr. Brady!

Intensive Therapy

Finally as my trembling and breathing subsided, I was able to make eye contact with Dr. Ansel, who handed me a tissue. Quietly and carefully he asked me, "Anne, can you tell me the name of the therapist?"

I shook my head no, explaining that I was worried about him and what he must be going through.

He responded intensely, "You are worried about him, Anne?"

When I told him that part of my problem was not being able to break off relationships with men—that I stayed stuck, he asked, "And did this therapist help you, Anne, with that problem?"

"No!" I said, starting to weep again.

"Anne," Dr. Ansel replied, "I understand now why you have been so afraid in therapy and I am so sorry that this has happened to you. You are going to need intensive therapy!"

I asked him if that meant getting locked in a sanitarium, a fear I had in the back of my mind over the years. He replied that they have not used that term since the 1940s, and that he did not know. He just needed to see me back in one week!

I had planned a trip to see a friend in Florida to get away from everything. We agreed that I would call him as soon as I returned. However, after four days in Florida I had to come home due to my frantic state of mind. At this time, I was starting to realize the full impact of what Dr. Brady had done to me!

After arriving home I immediately phoned Dr. Ansel for appointment, and as soon as I arrived at his office I breathlessly proclaimed, "My therapist whom I was involved with was Dr. Brady." Further, I declared, "I want to sue him." Feeling dazed, I added, "I can't believe I was having sex with him in his office. I feel like I have been living in another world and that I have been abused!"

"Indeed you have been abused, Anne," Dr. Ansel confirmed. He was happy I had finally opened up to him and was coming back to "reality."

He stated that I should find an attorney right away, adding that I deserved justice and a "piece of the pie." He had heard the news about Dr. Brady and that there were other female patients involved! Kindly, but strongly, Dr. Ansel told me that this was a serious case of malpractice, if not a crime.

Saturday the following day, when Dad's office was open in the morning, I dropped by to see my brother Eric again, to let him know what had happened. We were whispering in the lab when Dad appeared with a disgusted look on his face. He just knew, with his fatherly wisdom, what we were discussing. Dad looked at me with anger in his eyes and said sternly: "That is abuse and you should sue him!"

Although we had never said a word to him about any of it, I assumed that he put two and two together — from the newspapers and knowing how upset I had been the last few months — to conclude I was one of the women involved. I agreed with my father that I was going to sue.

I finally opened up and told him about the pregnancy and abortion. Eric and Dad both came over and hugged me. I felt such wonderful support and understanding from them! There was no blame on me. As doctors, they especially knew about the power of transference and counter-transference, along with issues of ethics and how crossing that boundary line amounted to extremely serious abuse and malpractice!

To Grieve

As if a deadly storm were whirling me around, I began sinking into the depths of more grief. At first I was filled with horror, shock, and guilt after the abortion and Dr. Brady abandoning me in the hotel, but now I was overwhelmed, confused, and had difficulty breathing. The denial I had was surfacing as I began breaking free of the horrific control he had of my mind for so many years, reality setting in so I could finally see what he had done to me!

Every Thursday night my daughter would call me from Berkeley to see how I was doing. It was difficult to hide the depth of my pain from the loss of the baby, along with the dreams I had for my children and marriage. I would express my deep love for her and Sean, telling her that no matter what happened, I would always love them!

Suicidal thoughts recurred at times; I just found the magnitude of all that had occurred too overwhelming! A couple of years later I would discover that Nadine was fully aware of this. At one point, Dr. Ansel made me promise him that I would not harm myself. "I can promise you for a week," I replied. I was seeing him weekly then!

One night I forced myself to write a letter to Dr. Brady over the pain he had caused. I angrily wrote of the terrible ways he had lied to me while taking advantage of me and sexually assaulting me. I especially pointed out to him how I was extremely distressed by the abortion! The child whom I loved so much within me was a part of us. "I wondered what ever happened to the sacredness of human life," I asked him. This was all that I could do at this point. I was unable to speak with him in person anymore, due to the impending lawsuit.

Wandering into a bookstore, I was drawn to some self-help and spiritual works by Kevin Keys and Louise Hay, which seek to help one achieve higher consciousness. They also enlightened me to an understanding of what was normal and abnormal in relationships. It was the beginning of awakening to another life as I immersed myself in these great books.

I also began attending the beautiful Self-Realization Temple again. It had been many years since I had been there. Their teachings, by

Paramahansa Yogananda, were of Eastern origin. Often I would stroll among their lovely meditation gardens atop beach cliffs. It was such a healing environment and another catalyst to help me cope!

After Nadine left for college, my son and I had to move to an apartment. It seemed like everything was in upheaval and changing in our lives. One early morning I awakened gasping for air. Leaving Sean, I immediately drove over to my parents' home. I quickly pulled out a paper bag and began breathing into it, while my mother was calling for dad. He came to console me and settled me down with his calm way, telling me to take very slow deep breaths. Then he handed me some cold water. My breathing subsided to a more normal pace.

My father explained that I was having panic attacks and that I should see Dr. Ansel, telling me that I had been a victim of rape, brainwashing, and abuse! I was unable to go to work, but that was the farthest thing from my mind. My only desire was to be home and safe.

I read in the newspaper of two other doctors who had been involved with their female patients. One of them hired a gunman as a scare tactic for the woman who was suing him. I couldn't help but become hyper-vigilant, wondering if someone would come after me, too. I simply didn't know who to trust anymore!

My grief and fear were affecting many levels of my life, but I knew deep down that I had to stand up and face whatever else was coming. I was determined to honor the life of my baby, my two children, and myself. I had to be strong in order to reveal all of the truth and bring Dr. Brady to justice—something I never fathomed would happen! It wasn't an easy decision because of the fact that he had been my lover, doctor, and father image for twenty years!

CHAPTER 13

SEARCHING FOR HELP

An Attorney

The first attorney I met was Dave in San Diego. He was very professional and knowledgeable of malpractice. His female legal Assistant as well, was compassionate. After hearing my story, they looked at each other and shook their heads. Dave apologized to me profusely upon realizing that he already had a client who had just begun a lawsuit against Dr. Brady for the same situation!

The attorney elaborated how Dr. Brady had conveyed the exact same sentiments to his client of wanting her to "bond with a man, and that it would be a secret relationship!" I was in total disbelief – it seemed unfathomable to me! He explained then that it would constitute a conflict of interest for him to take my case. His legal assistant said, "I hope this doctor loses every penny he has for what he has done!"

Luckily my father knew an excellent family attorney whom I could get advice from. Although he did not handle criminal cases of this type, he knew exactly whom to refer me to, an attorney in downtown San Diego who "took no prisoners" he told me.

"That sounds fine to me!" I angrily replied.

The following week I met with the attorney, Conrad, whose office was in a high-rise in downtown San Diego. He was keenly interested in my case, and within a week his firm served legal papers to Dr. Brady! It encompassed a pending lawsuit reading, "Donahue vs. Brady, for extreme sexual, emotional, and mental abuse over an eight-year period between 1980 and 1988." This would be the beginning of depositions, medical tests, and legal appointments over the next two-and-a-half years.

"The Good Old Boys"

After informing Dr. Ansel that I had finally found an excellent attorney and that Dr. Brady had been served with legal papers, he was very pleased! He also informed me that Dr. Brady was about to leave the area and wanted me to make sure I have a "piece of the pie."

Dr. Ansel began to further tell me that it would be in my best interest to have a separate psychiatrist for the legal matters. This was to ensure that my relationship with him would remain focused, just along the level of professional patient-client relationship. He pointed out the chance that I might have transference again. I realized this was best, as I now had more knowledge about healthy boundaries.

Thus began my search for another Psychiatrist to assist me on my legal case! Dr. Ansel sought out doctors in the La Jolla, San Diego, and the North county area but was unable to find *one* doctor who was willing to be involved. He explained that it had to do with the "brotherhood of physicians" sticking together, and that Dr. Brady was so well renowned in the area. I was dismayed at hearing this, which made me further realize just how naïve a woman I had really been!

Dr. Ansel made a promise to me that he would remain with me now for the duration of the trial — and continue to be my personal psychiatrist. He was such a wonderful ethical doctor whom I was beginning to respect more and more, someone who made me understand what doctor-patient relationships are truly about. Earlier, Dr. Ansel disclosed to me that he had been a student of Dr. Brady's at one time, and respected him then.

This made me realized what an enormous task it was for him to take my case on! He was a genuine psychiatrist/physician and a man of morals and courage. I was very humbled to know that he stood by my side. It would still be years, though, for me to understand all that was happening!

A Women's Group

Dr. Ansel referred me to a women's group in San Diego for more female support. It was small and very intimate, consisting of just five women. Some of the stories of abuse were very difficult to listen to.

One of the women had been strapped to a bed by her stepfather at five years old and repeatedly raped. This was unbelievable to me, describing a world I had never known! I asked if I could give her a hug but she refused, explaining she was not ready to be touched. Two of the other ladies whom I met in the group had also both been taken advantage of by their therapists, a polite way of saying they too "had been raped."

One, a tiny pretty blond, had gone to her doctor's home where he held his "therapy" with her. His wife stood watching as he coerced her into letting him penetrate her from behind, explaining that he was reenacting her father's abuse of her so that she could relive it and heal from it." The woman told me she too was very naïve. She had never been to therapy, having been married to the same man for twenty years. The last in the group was a lovely dark-haired woman who was made to dance seductively for her counselor, before sitting her on his lap having sex with her! This, too, occurred over several years and she was forced to have several abortions!

Sometimes I wondered why I was in this group: my case seemed less abusive at the time, until I was able to grasp the depth of its many dynamics years later!

The psychologist who led the women's group was kind with us, letting us open up at our own pace. We bonded together for the course of our journey until we felt we were ready to be on our own. It was the first time I could even manage a small group, since I had started legal proceedings a few months earlier. I had only been able to see Dr. Ansel one-on-one.

CHAPTER 14

Depositions and Tests

Being Deposed

It would be another two years before the trial. During this period, I was called in for depositions by Dr. Brady's attorneys. They asked me very personal questions pertaining to my relationship with Dr. Brady, like how many times we had sex in the office. This was irrelevant, as once was already considered malpractice!

I had researched the phenomenon of transference (discussed more in Chapter 17) while awaiting the trial, and had learned much about it as well from Dr. Ansel.

In transference, a patient views a psychiatrist as an important figure in their life, such as a father. The patient "transfers" this over to a doctor, not even realizing it. Dr. Ansel explained thus, "You could stand there naked and still the doctor holds the authority to protect the patient and not to violate her!" This was for the protection of the patient and the ethical practice of the therapist!

Dr. Brady retained three of the top attorneys from Los Angeles, the main one being a very tough female. He certainly needed them, as more women had surfaced claiming abuse by Dr. Brady. The female attorney questioned me using maneuvers to make me feel that I were to blame.

When she asked me if Dr. Brady had ever brought up marriage, I replied, "Yes." She then inquired if he had ever taken me out on a date or given me flowers. "Well, no," I said, then added, "but I had been to his home a few times — but no one knew as it was late in the evening." At the time I was oblivious as to why the flowers mattered.

Then there was the issue of how I knew that it was his baby. I couldn't believe this would be asked, as Dr. Brady knew very well that it was his baby! The lawyer suggested that a "friend of mine, Dick," may have been the father. Dr. Brady was the only one who could have told them this, which disgusted me! My friend was only an acquaintance, and in fact was encouraged by Dr. Brady! He had moved away a year earlier as well!

To my fear and dismay, in the next deposition Dr. Brady was sitting across from me! I began praying immediately, something that I did regularly since the abortion and abandonment by him! When his attorney asked me how many times we had sex in his office, I had to think for a few minutes, trying to remember over eight years, which was difficult in the moment. Finally I suddenly blurted out, "About sixty times!" and began laughing hysterically. I didn't know why I was laughing, perhaps it was because of the immense pressure!

I noticed Dr. Brady's face turning red with anger, his mouth clenched tightly and his previously soft eyes glaring at me with fire in them!

His attorneys and mine were all staring at me dumbfounded. Face somber, his female attorney asked for a recess and requested to continue the deposition another time.

My attorneys and I thus left the deposition room, then we all burst out laughing while running down the hall to their office. It was such a relief to laugh after so many months of intense questions. I'm sure they heard us, but we just could not hold back. When we sat down, finally catching our breaths, my attorney, Conrad, asked me if what I had declared was indeed true. I responded, "To the best of my knowledge," and added, "He often couldn't keep it up for long, either!" I was seething when I told him that. Conrad looked surprised, asking, "Really?" Then Kate, his assistant attorney, murmured: "Oh my God, I can't believe we are talking about this!" And we all began laughing again!

The next deposition was sad for me as his attorney asked me about my previous abortions, which made me feel guilty. She asked why the abortion with Dr. Brady's baby was any different to have affected me so much. I simply told her that they were all devastating, but this one more so as I had been involved and in love with Dr. Brady for many years, having known him in fact since I was nineteen. I also added my previous abortion was one of the main reasons I had gone in for counseling nine years ago. I was speaking softly at the remembrance of those years, but my heart was beating rapidly. The final year before the trial, my father, brother Eric, and my mother were also called in for depositions. The other side wanted to question them about their knowledge of events, their relationship with me, as well as Dr. Brady's. Again it was wonderful how my family stood up for me! They knew of my state of instability during the years I was secretly involved with Dr. Brady. My attorneys Conrad and Kate made sure to meet with them beforehand, to give them details of what would occur in the depositions.

I know that Dr. Brady's attorneys pressured my father into feeling guilty for not having spent more time with me developing a better emotional relationship, but Dad explained to them that he did the best he could with eight children and he was a very busy doctor. My mother simply went on about what a beautiful and good baby I was. She described how I used to sit on the sofa just staring at everything around me, then plopping onto the living room carpet. She was naïve as to depositions too. They eventually decided not to use Mother at the trial.

Eric took the depositions very hard. When they asked him if there were ever any family meetings, he responded, "Well, if there were I wasn't there!" I heard from his wife how disturbing it was for him after all of the personal questions. My mother was aghast at the whole process, remarking, "Someone should be with you, Anne, at these interrogations!" But I felt so strong then, as though I needed no one. It was my anger and faith that carried me through, and the need to honor my children and unborn baby — as well as myself.

Dr. Brady appeared desperate too, giving his lawyers personal information that was, at one time, supposed to be completely confidential!

The next question they asked my parents was if they had any knowledge of my two other abortions! My parents had only recently become aware of the one with Dr. Brady. My mother had told me, "It would have been a beautiful baby. Someone would have loved it!!

"That someone was me!" I had replied, upset!

She did not know the whole story at the time, and my parents had not been aware of my other two previous abortions. I could only reflect how — after all of the secrecy surrounding my pregnancies trying to hide something so beautiful — now everyone knew anyway! It all seemed so surreal!

Dr. Brady's attorneys even called for a deposition one of my girlfriends with whom I had disclosed my involvement with him. I had visited her when I was pregnant with his baby, and she was well aware of the situation. She too said the deposition was grueling and that they put her on the spot trying to turn things around as to the dates of when I had seen him last and other things besides. But being the strong woman she was, she stood up for the truth!

Forensic Doctors

Forensic doctors deal with the application of medical knowledge to establish facts in a civil or criminal case. By now I was deep in intensive counseling with Dr. Ansel, who continued to assist me as the legal proceedings unfolded. At one of my sessions with him, I burst out crying while running out of his office. It was becoming overwhelming going through counseling regarding my life and the reality of my abuse by Dr. Brady. Now I had to face forensic doctors for tests and intense questions.

But Dr. Ansel was extremely patient, kind, and professional! I could not have done it without his enormous support! This time, he was preparing for his own deposition, and he would be an "expert witness" too.

I continued to pray and trust in God that justice would prevail. As well, looming over my thoughts was the angelic presence that surrounded me in the hotel room with the message that I would become a powerful woman and sue Dr. Brady.

It continued to echo in my mind when I was all alone, wondering if I would live or die that night!

In Fairbanks Ranch I saw the first forensic doctor. While the session was recorded, he asked straightforward personal questions about my youth, education, first marriage, and religious beliefs. I assumed they would like to use the fact that my parents were Catholics. However, it was never my chosen faith, although I had grown to appreciate many facets of it. By now, I was no longer on any antidepressants or other medications.

Although I did well with support, my mind seemed to become slower under pressure. Subsequently, I was also interviewed by a compassionate Italian psychiatrist in La Jolla. His expertise was in criminal cases. He was quite sharp as to what had taken place, even to the point of saying, with disgust, "This is a criminal act, Anne. He violated you tremendously. I even feel he might have wanted you to take your own life that night in the hotel."

I was aghast at this, for in truth the thought had also crossed my mind. My voice began to crack, and the doctor kindly handed me a tissue. I was, however, heartened by the thought that he would be a forensic specialist in my case. My attorneys were proving to be excellent at finding amazing forensic doctors.

Next for me to see was an economist who would deal with my loss of income during the years I was involved with Dr. Brady.

First, he gave me a few tests relating to my memory and knowledge of the present and past. I thought they were rather easy, except when he asked me who the current president was. It took my mind a while to recall and sort the question out. I remember saying, "The peanut man," all the while feeling embarrassed and blushing at not knowing the president's name right away — though I finally did recall that President Bush was then in office.

When he took me into another room to do some written questions, a clock near me made me jump when I heard it ring. The economist asked me if I did that often. I replied: "Yes, I have become very jumpy and startle easily." For this and several other reasons, he concluded that I was suffering from posttraumatic stress disorder (PTSD). I did not really understand the depth of this at the time, or what it meant.

Finally, I had to see a female psychiatrist at UCLA. She was a very kind and intelligent woman — and extremely clear as to the malpractice and abuse by Dr. Brady. She was appalled at the number of years we were involved and that he had even seen my children a few times! She was concerned for their welfare at being alone with Dr. Brady. That had never crossed my mind, I told her, as I had trusted him. Fortunately this was not the case!

Being at the top of her field, she would be a wonderful expert witness. During the deposition with Dr. Brady's attorneys, she showed no qualms or hesitation to speak up for the patient and their rights. She was adamant that it was the physician—especially being seventeen years older and well renowned—who used his power of authority and transference over me! This amazing female doctor never let the other side get away with any obscure questions or manipulations!

Dr. Brady's Depositions

Dr. Brady had already been deposed by my attorneys alone, then a couple of times with his own attorneys present. I was not able to sit in the room, nor did I want to. I learned from Kate, though, that my medical chart, which had been kept locked in his office desk, was very scant. After several years of seeing him, there was little information in it.

This they thought was improper in itself. Conrad and Kate also discovered that Dr. Brady had attempted to put me on disability. When they asked why, his only reply was to help me receive benefits. They then asked him if he thought that I was ill? He nervously replied "No."

He was also put on the spot when my attorneys asked why, after so many years, I had not improved on personal issues like finances, relationships, and cognitive behavior. He could not answer. When they probed on my diagnosis, he merely blamed it on "premenstrual syndrome." Again a question was asked about sex in the office, and he quietly said, "Just a handful of times!"

On his last deposition I was requested to be in the room, which made me edgy! I was right across from Dr. Brady, but thankfully Kate sat beside me. She handed Dr. Brady a letter, asking him to read it out loud for all to hear.

Somewhat under his breath, he slowly read the referral letter that he had mailed to Dr. Ansel. It read that he could no longer see me as a patient because I was having romantic feelings toward him. He then stated that he had not been able to help me advance over the last eight years.

He noted that I came from a large Catholic family, with a mother who had a "mental health issue." He indicated he had been her doctor, as well, for many years. Then Dr. Brady asked Dr. Ansel if he would see me as his patient.

I realized my mother had a mental health challenge at times, and she had her own ways. It had been somewhat confusing for some of us over the years but despite this, she was beloved by the family and many others. To hear the words from Dr. Brady thus was upsetting, as he had never relayed details of her diagnosis to me in "therapy." I pondered that she may have been overmedicated as well, even misdiagnosed perhaps! And why would he seduce and take advantage of me if he was aware this?

Finally Kate asked Dr. Brady why he suddenly moved to another town. "There was more opportunity for me there," he replied. It was difficult for me to fathom that he just suddenly moved from his home in La Jolla for this reason. No doubt he was just being shrewd enough to plan this for some time. In my eyes, he definitely wanted to run from his indiscretions!

Before the Trial

The final appointment I had three weeks before the trial would be my most difficult! A highly regarded doctor at a hospital in San Diego, he specialized in victims of sexual assault — a category I never imagined I would ever fit in! A psychologist, he was very personable, sensitive, listened intently, and seemed to go out of his way to treat me like a lady. He was already aware of my case and upcoming trial.

In truth I was wearing down, unable to see Dr. Ansel for some time now for my regular visits from lack of money. Nevertheless, I tried to keep a front on with my smile. The doctor began the tests with flashcards. Each card bore a picture and I was to tell him the first thing that came to my mind. The images were colorful - some like flowers I would say, another a hospital, then a child, a uterus, a baby, another uterus, and an abortion.... My lips then began to quiver and I started to cry, as it brought up such emotional trauma for me.

I managed to hear him ask me, "How many abortions have you had, Anne?"

I could not answer, feeling somehow trapped, and I broke down in a flood of tears. After a while I stammered, "I might have lost the beautiful photo of my two children and me," while searching through my purse frantically. "It is all that I have — I just need to find it!"

The doctor became quiet. Intensely looking at me with concern he said, "That will be all the testing today, Anne." He proceeded to inquire when I had last seen Dr. Ansel. Nervously I replied that it had been three weeks, admitting that I did not have enough money to go for a visit. I explained that Dr. Ansel expected to be paid each time.

Calmly he insisted I should see my counselor and proceeded to phone Dr. Ansel. Failing this, he continued, "If Dr. Ansel won't see you, then I will — without any charge." He thought I should stay there at the hospital and be admitted that night even!

Anxiously I told him: "Oh, no, my children are at home and I have to be there!" Then I thanked him for his graciousness.

"Do you have anyone who can pick you up?" he queried, adding, "Because I do not feel comfortable letting you drive home in the state you're in!"

I hesitated, thinking of my parents, but felt that I had been enough of a burden and didn't want to involve them anymore. My best girlfriend was sick, my grandma had died. I could not think of anyone else at that time, so I simply thanked him. Having calmed down, I reassured him that I would be all right then.

Finally he agreed to let me leave but was careful to remind me, "Please drive slowly all the way home, Anne, and call me when you arrive." I told him that I would.

Although I never saw him again, I did discover later that he shared information with my attorneys, especially pointing out his impression of me as a good mother. Further, he indicated he was willing to be an expert witness if needed.

It was already dark out when I left the doctor's office. I was exhausted. The drive was about 30 minutes from San Diego but I did make it home, though very shaken. So much had happened and it all seemed to be hitting me particularly harder a couple of months before the trial. Walking through the door I hugged my wonderful children, who had been diligently doing their homework. It was so comforting to see Nadine and Sean this distinctly difficult night. I telephoned the doctor, letting him know I did make it home.

Right after sitting down near the children on our sofa, I began drifting off to sleep.

The following morning, Dr. Ansel phoned. He sounded a bit perturbed, mentioning how the forensic doctor described how upset I had been the night before during our meeting. Dr. Ansel told me that I should have told him, adding that he would see me on a contingency basis until the trial.

All along my desire had been to remain with Dr. Ansel, as I had already gone that far with him. It was quite heartwarming, however, to finally find other doctors who really cared and understood the dynamics of mental and sexual abuse by a psychiatrist!

Calling Chad

A couple of days before the trial, Dr. Ansel prepared his case as an expert witness. He wanted to know the exact date of my breakup with Chad, my boyfriend before I started therapy with Dr. Brady. By this time, I could not remember precisely. Anxiously I decided to call Chad. He sounded reticent upon hearing my voice at first, but he maintained vivid memory about our breakup.

He chose the moment to confide that he had mourned the loss of our baby. It was a touching moment sharing our sorrow together. Chad then said, "I imagine you must have felt abandoned by the doctor too?"

"Yes, I had, in several ways," I confirmed.

Chad intimated that he was teaching children Christianity at his church. I shared with him that I had found my own faith, too. He then declared, "Anne, you will win the case against that doctor!"

CHAPTER 15

THE TRIAL

The Courtroom

T he Superior Court of San Diego was distinctly quiet and serene as two opposing groups of litigants made their way into it. The walls were carved of dark wood, which resonated with an old and established — almost sacred — place. It felt so surreal. I wondered what this place held in store for me, though I felt very strongly with my Spirit that truth was on my side.

Sitting near the right side of the judge's empty bench was Dr. Brady with his attorneys. They appeared to be reviewing their documents while speaking to one another. I promptly stopped looking in their direction once I had seen them.

A motley crowd sat in the back rows behind us to observe the proceedings. I assumed some of them were law students, while the others were just curious. My father and Eric were to come the next day, my attorneys thinking it would be a while before they were called. It was almost nine o'clock in the morning when we suddenly heard the court clerk announce: "Please rise" as the judge walked in and sat down.

Conrad had suggested that I wear something simple, so I wore my cream-colored skirt with a matching long-sleeved blouse. We were seated in the front center, still some distance away from the judge, as there had to be room for discussions and arguments. Thankfully I was sitting in-between my two wonderful lawyers Kate and Conrad, Kate on my right and Conrad on my left. Dr. Ansel and Nadine were patiently waiting outside the courtroom to be called in as witnesses.

Opening Statements

There were to be opening statements by lawyers from both sides to explain why we were there. I noticed that more observers had quietly entered the back of the courtroom. My side was to prove that Dr. Brady had committed *immense negligence* as a doctor becoming sexually involved with me from 1980 to 1988 and ending with a pregnancy and forced abortion. Specifically, Conrad opened with: "We will show serious *sexual, mental, and emotional* harm to my client. This is cause for negligence and medical malpractice."

Twisted Truth

The defense declared that they would show "Anne had been seeing another man who may have been the true father of the baby."

Again, I was in shock at this outright lie! As well, the female attorney went on to say that I did not come forward right away until I heard of other women who were involved with Dr. Brady."

Having heard of the term "legal system tactics" and of lawyers who twisted the truth or lied just to win a case, I knew then that I was seeing live ones. I looked over in disbelief at Dr. Brady who was going over notes with his attorney, when suddenly he turned around and looked right at me! Our once loving eyes locked and I knew he saw the shocked look of disbelief on my face at these comments. I had always trusted him and somehow I knew he could feel this! Then he turned quickly. I decided to sue him when I finally realized all his untruths, and after the trauma from the assault and forced abortion! Even then it was an extremely difficult decision to do as I had known and loved him for twenty years as my doctor, lover, and "father image."

Witnesses

The first witness called was Dr. Ansel. He came in giving me a warm smile. He had been such a source of support for me it was so endearing, and now he even chose to stand up against one of his colleagues for me. My faith in humanity was growing again, even amidst all this turmoil.

Starting the proceedings, Conrad asked Dr. Ansel to describe what I was like when he first met me.

"Well, he started, "she was extremely nervous and scared. She had to ask me for a glass of water on her first visit. Then she told me that she had had an abortion five days earlier. Anne initially made up a story, contrived with Dr. Brady's encouragement, that the father of the baby was a lawyer." At this, a round of chuckles rippled in the courtroom. He continued, "After counseling therapy for four months with me, in October she admitted that it was in fact Dr. Brady's baby. At that she became quite hysterical, even to the point of having difficulty breathing."

Conrad followed up with, "To your knowledge, has Anne had any other male relationships for the last two years?"

Dr. Ansel shook his head while replying firmly, "No, she certainly has not," adding, "She has been in intensive counseling and could not be in a group situation either. Nor did she have any desire to be in another relationship."

Conrad asked Dr. Ansel if he could explain a little more about my therapy.

"It is like peeling an onion. The therapist starts with the top layer until the patient feels comfortable to move on. Anne had several layers to peel off, beginning with the years she did not receive proper treatment from Dr. Brady. We had to go back over many incidences of that relationship. There was her childhood, and her marriage and children were involved as well. This is the main process of healing in therapy."

"Have you come to a conclusion about Anne's diagnosis?" Conrad asked further.

"Oh, yes," Dr. Ansel replied. "First of all she suffers from posttraumatic stress disorder, brought on by her sexual relationship with Dr. Brady. She has major depressive disorder, which I am sure was exacerbated by his treatment of her as well."

"And how much longer do you feel Anne will need therapy?" Conrad next asked him.

"I feel she will need another two years of intensive therapy to understand and deal with what has happened to her. As of now she has serious trust issues with people. Additionally, she had to deal with her other diagnoses," Dr. Ansel concluded.

My daughter Nadine was the next witness. She had flown from Berkeley to testify for me. Nadine was such a strong and wonderful young lady, and my attorneys felt she would be an excellent witness. She committed to it without hesitation. Nadine proudly put her hand on the bible while swearing to "tell the whole truth and nothing but the truth." Warmth of love ran through me when we saw one another. More attentive now, the jurors focused on this smart young college girl.

They seemed to be behind her with kindness and understanding in their eyes of how difficult all of this must be for her!

The female defense attorney asked her a few questions pertaining to her understanding of my relationship with Dr. Brady. As well, she asked if she was aware of the reason she was called as a witness. Nadine answered yes, and that she understood what the case was about. They proceeded to inquire about her background and she proudly responded, "My mother is a loving single mother who had been employed as a practical nurse. I attended Carlsbad High and am now a second year student at the University of California at Berkeley majoring in political science."

Suddenly the defense attorney rose and asked her about the men I had dated. Nadine replied: "She hasn't dated anyone in years."

"And how do you know this, Nadine?" the attorney insisted.

Nadine quickly and firmly replied, "Because she was home with us every night!"

The courtroom became eerily quiet after her testimony.

By now I had begun quietly weeping from the intense session! The tears were uncontrollable, but I tried to hide them. I so wanted to get up and hug her. It did not seem fair that she was on the stand and not me! But I felt timid not knowing what to do. The judge made a motion to Kate, who immediately pulled out a Kleenex for me. I just put it over my eyes with my head down!

Nadine went on to state that I phoned her every Thursday night to talk. "Mom would tell me how much she loved me and no matter what happened, she wanted me to know that! I could tell by the tone in her voice that she was contemplating suicide or at least wanting to die."

When I heard this horrible acknowledgement coming from her, I let out a loud gasp. Through the corner of my eyes, I could see the jury staring at me. Nadine and I were both crying at this point, along with some of the jurors! It was overwhelming to think of what we had both been through for so many years. Our eyes met with so much love and pain as we wept together!

Soon, Dr. Brady's attorney concluded her questioning with "That will be all."

Nadine rose from the bench and walked toward the back of the courtroom still crying and holding a Kleenex that a juror had handed her with a supportive smile. I felt so sad wanting to hold my sweet daughter but couldn't. I was reluctant making a scene—I did not know the court protocol and I felt as though I were on trial too.

Settlement?

Gratefully the attorneys and judge requested a recess for two hours. When they returned, we were asked to consider a settlement for 250,000.

At first I refused, feeling I deserved a minimum of $500,000. In fact I had been told by a therapist that I would receive at least 1 million. It just didn't seem fair after so many years of his entrapment, and neither did it seem fair to my children who were deeply affected by his abuse.

Dr. Ansel and I sat outside the courtroom discussing the settlement offer during the break. He admitted that it would be better to have "a bird in the cage than none at all." I heard that in order to pay the settlement, one of many I presumed, Dr. Brady had to ask his mother for the money against her own home mortgage. After another hour discussing it with Dr. Ansel and my attorneys, who confirmed "There's just no more money," I decided to settle. I found out that Dr. Brady had finally admitted to his lawyers his guilt.

Later, I recalled Dr. Brady had conveyed to me that he had given his money to his brother for safekeeping, just before he moved and when I had still trusted him. It didn't matter now, I only wanted completion. Still, it was amazing how he had managed to publish a book, relocate, and begin a new career during the interim before the trial!

I left to go to the ladies room and on my return, as I was about to open the courtroom doors, I heard someone call out my name from the hallway. I waited by the door until the caller arrived. It was Dr. Brady. Out of reflex a smile came over me for a moment seeing him, before I recovered and reminded myself that I was not to speak or have any interaction with him.

"It will be all right, Anne," he said, smiling. He acted as if everything would be back to normal with the settlement. He appeared to exude guilt and own up to his responsibility but I said nothing, slightly nodding my head and quickly returning to my chair by my attorneys.

When I told Dr. Ansel about my encounter with Dr. Brady, he looked disgusted, saying, "What an egocentric person he is." I then realized what the term "God complex" meant.

In time we all rose and the honorable judge addressed the courtroom, informing everyone that a settlement had been reached. He asked me if I had anything to say. With a blank face I replied "No." I could not begin to fathom what else I could possibly say. With that we were all dismissed.

My attorneys, daughter, Dr. Ansel, and some of the jurors gathered outside the courtroom doors. Beside us stood Dr. Brady with his briefcase, as though he were going to join us.

No one bothered to look at him, but I could see him through the corner of my eyes. Looking around with a little smile in his face, he proceeded to take his briefcase and left.

I felt very safe with Dr. Ansel and my attorneys, all of whom I had been so close with the last two-and-a-half years. I so appreciated all that they had done to help me regain some of my self-respect and bring Dr. Brady to justice.

One juror expressed the view that it was easy to see how my case could happen between any doctor and patient. This was astounding and hurtful, but it made me realize the ignorance and misunderstanding some people could have regarding the phenomenon of transference, brainwashing, and sexual assault—not to mention the years of devastating affects it could have on patients and families!

Looking away from the group I saw Dr. Brady walking alone down the courthouse hallway, briefcase in hand, vanishing before my eyes. He had lost his license, pride, and some money. With me, I was just relieved that it was finally all over....

CHAPTER 16

FRAGMENTED

Aftershocks

After the trial my attorney handed me a check for $5,000.00. "The rest will be mailed to you, Anne, after we have paid all fees and deducted our percentage," he told me. I immediately used the money to purchase necessities for my children and began planning a move back to Carlsbad, where we could be closer to my family and Sean's high school.

The settlement fee was cut in half by the time all the legal and medical fees were paid. I purchased lovely new furniture, immersed myself decorating our new home and loved every minute of it.

Nadine was particularly affected by the trial. She even felt sorry for Dr. Brady at first. After all, he had been part of our lives for many years. The aftershocks for both of us were unexpected and extremely difficult. Needing to recover from the emotional strain of the trial, Nadine took a semester off Berkeley.

The house wasn't even mine—I only rented it. All of the pretty things were comforting for a while, but I began to feel eerily alone, that something was drastically missing. It was my self that didn't really come "alive." I wasn't sure who I was anymore, having been attached to Dr. Brady half my lifetime, and the future I had hoped for dissipated.

I began to dissociate, not totally in touch with reality at times, finding myself needing to go to a "room in my mind" in order to feel safe! *What is happening to me?* I anxiously thought. Thinking that the settlement would be my answer to healing, I didn't return to See Dr. Ansel for counseling as he had suggested. After the emotional turmoil brought about by recent events, I found it upsetting to bring myself to see any more psychiatrists or doctors.

Running

To calm myself I decided to travel, first visiting Catalina Island. I so wanted to be alone and away from everything at this time. I had a wonderful and much needed break in the beginning of December. Stepping off the boat onto the island, I was welcomed by the sight of the townspeople decorating their enormous Christmas tree, the multicolored lights reflecting off the bay making it serendipitous!

The Catalina Hotel I was staying in was atop a rugged hill overlooking the harbor. It offered a splendid view of the yachts rocking in the water below.

This is like a story book! I thought. In the evening I strolled into a fine restaurant on the water with beautiful music softly playing in the background. Memories of my early times with Dr. Brady still imbedded in my mind made my eyes misty. I still startled easily, and at times I thought I saw a glimpse of him! In some strange way, I seemed to be looking for Dr. Brady....

Still all I could think of was getting away. I took my daughter to Cancun for her high school graduation gift. It was amazing seeing the emerald rainforest from the small commuter plane. We had never done anything like this before and it was so special to spend quality time with Nadine.

When she returned to college, I traveled to Utah. Longing to be alone in nature to heal and find myself again, I enjoyed a cabin on Robert Redford's property "Sundance" high in the mountains. While horseback riding through trails and pine trees, I found myself suddenly amongst gorgeous waterfalls and streams! A rainbow often glistened through the sun and water. It was like being in heaven, if only for a little while!

Finally I returned to Carlsbad to be with Sean in our new home. I was tired of traveling now, and the money was dwindling fast. Fortunately Sean had taken a job in town at an upscale restaurant, as I still felt unable to return to work. It was just so wonderful to be able to give him a nice home where his friends could visit.

PTSD

Shortly after arriving home from my travels, I began having flashbacks of being with Dr. Brady on his office floor having sex, sometimes with his hand over my mouth so no one could hear us. It now felt like rape to me. The flashbacks would come at different times, triggered by a person, loud noise, or a baby crying. Nightmares also intruded my life frequently, of Dr. Brady coming after me and killing our infant! I would wake up perspiring, my heart beating rapidly as I jumped out of bed to see where I was and what was happening. Then I would become more aware, realizing that I was safe at home.

Early one morning I awakened having difficulty breathing, so I raced over to my parents' home not far away. Gasping for air I told my mother I could not breathe, as I began reaching for a brown paper bag to breath into. Mom immediately ran to find my father. Shortly he entered the room speaking calmly to me. Breathlessly I told him how scared I was, that Dr. Brady might come after me and my family—that I couldn't sleep and had rapid heartbeats with shortness of breath.

I thought I was having a heart attack, but Dad knew I was instead having panic attacks. He did take my pulse and listened to my heart while asking me the usual questions, if one were having a heart attack. After settling me down, he advised me to see Dr. Ansel for counseling.

"It takes time to recover from such a horrible ordeal, Anne," he said. "You just went through what amounted to rape and abuse, and you have progressive PTSD." He was very concerned about me. *Dad was always there for us*, I thought, *isn't that what men and doctors do – protect women?* Mom too was very frightened.

Grieve for Whom?

Returning to Dr. Ansel, I narrated to him that I had been traveling on and off for a few months, had moved, and changed my last name for privacy and safety reasons. I recounted moments I was "looking" for Dr. Brady in my mind while being terrified of what had happened! I still couldn't believe that I was having sex with him in his office. *We had had a bond*, I thought, *but it wasn't real*. For the first time I admitted to Dr. Ansel seeing my sexual past with Dr. Brady in a new light: "I feel that I have been raped while locked in a closet for eight years." I was shaking, unable to absorb it all!

Dr. Ansel explained that panic attacks were inherent in people suffering from posttraumatic stress disorder, which, in my case, intensified once the trial was over. He imparted that I had begun a deep mourning process over Dr. Brady's loss and the realization of the assault, all of which helped confound my sense of identity. He decided I had to go back on an antidepressant.

This reminded me of the women's assault group which I had attended again after the trial. I was not able to speak at first, but after a time I managed to say that I had won the case, suddenly blurting out, "I feel like my father just died." I then gasped while waving my arms around, trying to speak again but was unable to. The group leader quietly said, "It is okay to cry, Anne," at which point I burst into tears of relief. It proved to be a safe place for me as everyone was so supportive. They too had tears in their eyes then.

I thought about how Dr. Brady who had been like a father to me for twenty years. I always took it for granted that a man, and especially a doctor, was supposed to protect a woman. Intellectually I've gained ground, but still some parts remained monumental for me to take in, as though I were grieving for the loss of three different people—a father, lover, and doctor.

A few weeks into seeing Dr. Ansel again, we uncovered the root of my delayed grief.

For that, we needed to go back to the very reason I had gone to Dr. Brady in 1980: *because **I had lost the relationship with Chad and our baby**. Reeling from this loss, I had transferred my needs over to Dr.*

Brady instead of allowing the grief to run through its entire natural course in the first place.

It finally became clear to me why I felt so fragmented and why I was suffering from PTSD the whole time. It was as though I had been in a state of limbo, waiting to recover while acting out my needs of marriage and a baby with Dr. Brady over eight years. I effectively put my whole life on hold! I had gone to him for help while trusting him, but the help never came because he deftly saw to it that I became obliviously seduced and lost in the vacuum of his mind.

Having to face the loss of Dr. Brady later, along with my forgotten youth and dreams, confounded my situation. No amount of money could have healed these emotional wounds; within a year, the money I had "won" was gone.

Regrettably, after the trial I did not take the time to heal, go to therapy, and understand everything that had occurred. The emotional impact was so enormous that I ran away. But mourning haunted me wherever I went. Further — and to my dismay — I came to understand the deeper impact this had on my children and our relationship. Being so confused, I had disrupted their own lives and was not there emotionally for them as I had once been.

If only I could turn back the clock and make it all right. But it was too late. Nadine was now in college and Sean too would soon be leaving.

CHAPTER 17

SEX WITH THERAPISTS

Rape

The power of authority figure is an intensely strong aphrodisiac. Sometime around 1990, I discovered an extremely informative and important book, *Sex in the Forbidden Zone*, written by Dr. Peter Rutter. This was a great aid for me in attempting to comprehend more fully the psychological processes at work during the time I was under Dr. Brady's control. It proved instructive information about the emotions that I similarly manifested.

Excerpts from the Book:

- *The forbidden zone is a condition of a relationship in which sexual behavior is prohibited, because a man holds in trust the intimate, wounded, vulnerable, or underdeveloped parts of a woman.*

- *The trust drives from the professional role of the man as doctor, therapist, lawyer, clergy, teacher or mentor.*
- *This creates an expectation that whatever parts of herself the woman entrusts to him (her property, body, mind, or spirit) must be used solely to advance her interests and will not be used to his advantage, sexual or otherwise.*
- *My position is that any sexual behavior by a man in power within what I define as the "forbidden zone" is inherently exploitive of a woman's trust.*
- *Because he is the keeper of that trust, it is the man's responsibility, no matter what the level of provocation or apparent consent by the woman, to assure that sexual behavior does not take place!*
- *Rape is the commission of sexual intercourse forcibly and without consent. The law has come to recognize that unless a person is psychologically free to say either yes or no, consent cannot be given, even if at the time of the sex act the person says yes.*
- *A man in this position of trust and authority becomes unavoidably a parent figure and is charged with the ethical responsibilities of the parenting role.*

- *Violations of these boundaries…,
  psychologically speaking, not only [effectively
  constitute acts of] rape but also acts of incest.*

This is so deep and true, and I know that it can also apply to men, not just women.

Another very enlightening work, *The Psychology of the Transference by* Carl Jung, states that within the transference dyad both participants typically experience a variety of opposites; that in love and in psychological growth, the key to success is the ability to endure the tension of the opposites without abandoning the process, and that this tension allows one to grow and to transform!"

Abuse of Mind, Body, Heart, Spirit

It isn't only the body that can be seduced, the mind as well can be manipulated. This gross abuse is all encompassing of the Spirit! Never in my life did I ever imagine that I — a mother, practical nurse, and doctor's daughter — would ever fall prey to such a devastating, unethical, demeaning assault and violation of the sacred trust of a psychiatrist!

The emotional imprint of this assault leaves an impact on people's lives for many years — some estimates put it at twenty years — that being under its overwhelming spell has been likened to having been a *prisoner of war* — with the same repercussions! The commission of this crime constitutes an extreme misuse of power, and transference can happen to anyone of any gender, age, or level of intelligence.

All the information finally led me to conclude that perhaps Dr. Brady had wanted me to die, as the good forensic doctor had intimated. Obviously he was well aware of the crime he had committed, otherwise he would not have attempted to cover up his actions by forcing me to have the abortion, making up a number of lies when referring me to Dr. Ansel and at the trial. My mind just couldn't stop drifting back to that episode wherein he totally abandoned me in the hotel room!

Only by the intervention of the angelic presence, prayers, meditations, and of having a female counselor years later could I attempt some semblance of wholeness again.

A Doctor's Vow, an Oath

Still hanging in my father's office is a framed "Hippocratic Oath" given to him by his sister upon his graduation from medical school. It was written in beautiful gold calligraphy. This embodies the sacred trust for patients. Below is the original *Hippocratic Oath* taken by doctors:

"My Beloved Father".

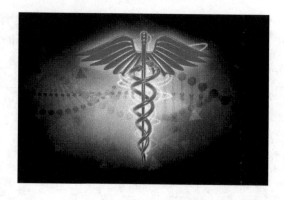

"Medical Cross"

The Hippocratic Oath

"I swear by Apollo the Physician, and Asclepius, and Hygieia and Panacea and all the gods and goddesses as my witnesses, that, according to ability and judgment, I will keep this Oath and this contract. To hold him who taught me this art equally dear to me as my parents, to be a partner in life with him, and to fulfill his needs when required; to look upon his offspring as equals to my own siblings, and to teach them this art, if they shall wish to learn it, without fee or contract; and that by the set rules, lectures, and every other mode of instruction, I will impart a knowledge of the art To my own sons, and those of my teachers, and to students bound by this contract and having sworn this oath to the law of medicine, but to no others. I will use those dietary regimens which will benefit my patients according to my greatest ability and judgment, and I will do no harm or injustice to them. I will not give a lethal drug to anyone if I am asked, nor will I advise such a plan : and similarly I will not give a woman a pessary to cause an abortion.

In purity and according to divine law I carry my life and my art. I will not use the knife, even upon those suffering from stones, but I will leave this to those who are trained in this craft. Into whatever homes I go, I will enter them for benefit of the sick, avoiding any voluntary act of impropriety or corruption, including the seduction of women or men, whether they are free men or slaves. Whatever I see or hear in the lives of my patients whether in connection with my professional practice or not, which ought not to be spoken of outside, will keep secret, as considering all such things to be private. So long as I maintain this Oath faithfully and without corruption, may it be granted to me to partake of life fully and the practice of my art, gaining respect of all men for all time. However, should I transgress this

Oath and violate it, may the opposite be my fate.

Touching on the core principles of the medical profession, this oath calls on all physicians to treat their practice as *singularly sacred,* infused with a spiritual mandate and divine law.

A more modern rendition of the oath reflects the same values while adding the consideration of dignity as indicated below.

The Physician's Oath

- *I solemnly pledge myself to consecrate my life to the service of Humanity;*
- *I will give to my teachers the respect and gratitude which is their due;*
- *I will practice my profession with conscience and dignity; the health of my patient will be my Number One consideration;*
- *I will maintain, by all the means in my power, the honor and the noble traditions of the medical profession; my colleagues will be my brothers;*
- *I will not permit considerations of religion, nationality, race, party politics, social standing, or sexual orientation to intervene between my duty and my patient;*
- *I will maintain the utmost respect for human life from the time of conception, even under threat, I will not use my medical knowledge contrary to the laws of humanity;*

- *I make these promises solemnly, freely, and upon my honor.*

In 1989, before the trial, I attended a "Victims of Crime" meeting in Sacramento. While we were on the subject of *sex between doctors and patients,* I recounted my particular case as a patient. Around 1992, it did become a crime for any doctor to engage in sex with a patient. If the act ever occurred, it would be considered rape.

CHAPTER 18

VANISHED IDENTITY

It Didn't Happen to Me

Despite the unrelenting emotional tempest, my mind stubbornly demanded that I remain in denial, presenting a façade of unreality that said, "It didn't happen to me!"

However, one can run but never truly hide. Ultimately your scars will surface, your actions will be limited, your self-esteem will be crushed even further, and your relationships will remain tumultuous. You may choose to remain isolated in "your own little world" away from life, but this choice leaves open the high probability that you will submerse yourself in alcohol or drugs. Also, with PTSD comes major depression. One could become homeless, or unfortunately choose suicide. I implemented some of these tactics as I attempted to circumvent the truth.

The years that I was exploited by Dr. Brady created a colossal chasm in my life, leaving me lost in time. Feeling uncomfortable in my nice clothes I threw most of them out, then shopped at consignment stores for simple replacements. Reclaiming my memory and true identity was similar to a personal battle with amnesia, but I slowly made progress even if it came in layers and pieces over the next twenty years. Having PTSD made it more complicated: I was immersed in fear wherever I went! It was as though I was held captive by Dr. Brady away from myself, children, family, and my own future. I finally came to see him as a twisted psychiatrist who simply wanted his way and insisted it would be under his duress!

A Shaman

Five years after the trial in 1995, I attended a seminar at church held by a retired ob-gyn. Years before, he relinquished Western medicine in order to become a spiritual shaman instead. After the seminar, I contacted him to obtain spiritual advice. When we met for lunch in Del Mar, he mentioned that he had been well known in his previous medical field. I recounted my own experience with Dr. Brady, especially pointing out that he didn't really heal me.

The doctor intimated that he well knew of Dr. Brady.

When I asked him later if he would kindly remove the term "therapeutic" to describe abortion—because it was not *therapeutic*, but rather quite damaging to the mother and child in so many horrific ways, including spiritual—he apologized profusely but explained that it was too late for him to do that.

Putting his head in his hands and looking down, he began to meditate. After a few minutes he gazed up at me, tears streaming down his face, telling me that Dr. Brady had loved me and this was my healing. Momentarily it confused me, wondering if it were true. He then added that I was in my prime and was "like Marilyn Monroe."

"Oh no," I said, "I do not see myself that way!"

Completely taking me off guard, he quietly shared with me that he had to leave his practice as he also had been involved with women. He had to ask me, "Do you know how difficult it is to be around beautiful women who admire you so much?"

His revelations had me totally dumbfounded. I guess I had stirred something up deep within him until I truly felt saddened for him.

I thanked him for the lunch and visit. On my way I resolved I would just have to move on and take care of myself!

Healing

As my awakening continued emerging from deep within my heart and soul, I found "shelter" in the arms of a loving massage therapist in Encinitas. Tender and intuitive, she would place a bouquet of flowers on my abdomen after each massage. The first time she did this I broke into tears—I was so touched. Her unconditional love was awesome, needed, and much appreciated!

I continued meditations at the *Self-Realization Temple* in Encinitas. Their wonderful messages kept me grounded with myself, God, and my feminine spirit. Its beautiful tropical gardens and ponds resplendent with colorful koi fish transported my soul to a higher realm of love!

Soon I took up classes at *Unity Church* centered on the metaphysical and without dogma. This opened up another spiritual door to personal growth and healing. Here I discovered the *Course in Miracles* (Foundation for Inner Peace), which became my utmost channel of true love and peace from God. It transformed my perception of the world, myself, and people! *The course* was in fact the only way I, with limited income, could receive the help I needed at the time.

At times I would visit a minister over my issues and grief of the past from the abortions and those mistakes I had made. The minister would remind me that there is a loving and all-forgiving God!

Journaling was a tool I began consistently after meeting Dr. Ansel when I was thirty-eight. It has always been a deeply rewarding experience. When one puts their heart into what is true on paper, it becomes a work of art, prayer, and enlightenment!

These uplifting experiences became a process of healing the Feminine, especially when I abruptly left therapy with Dr. Ansel again, to find myself. It opened my eyes to happiness along with solid, trustworthy people. All of these amazing spiritual experiences resonated with me as an individualized expression of God that I am, and began to heal my heart and soul!

An Apparition

During the writing of this chapter, I had an apparition one morning around 5:00 AM. Upon opening my eyes, I clearly saw another glowing golden cross right in front of me. I quietly gazed at it with awe while thanking the Holy Spirit, then said prayers. The beautiful cross remained for about 2 minutes, then disappeared. I suddenly realized that it was THANKSGIVING MORNING 2015! I called my sister Peggy and told her what had happened. We couldn't help but cry together as I spoke. She told me that I had had an "apparition." It was another vision I knew. I felt that the meaning for me was faith, trust, and devotion!

I recalled twenty-five years earlier when I saw and heard the angelic presence in the hotel room! I was so grateful to God this time. I also remembered that my grandmother had visions from the higher realms. She was a very spiritual lady whom I was close to!

Trying to Adjust

While continuing my metaphysical studies and practices during the 1990s, I took temporary jobs before returning to my familiar career in practical nursing, believing it would bring more stability into my life. However, after a couple of years I would either leave a position or be terminated.

I just wasn't the same person anymore. My coping skills had become limited, I had difficulty with concentration, and I continually suffered from anxiety and fatigue! Sleeping in my car during lunch was how I made it through the day. Moving was also common. I found rooms for rent with kind older women from my church, for economic reasons and in order to feel safe! Spending alone time studying my spiritual classes and practicing meditation made me feel safe so I could continue moving forward.

For a few months I found refuge at my parents' home, where I slept for long periods of time. Finally my father gave me a new mild antidepressant, which helped and enabled me to move to a condo still attempting to reclaim myself. Nadine sweetly suggested I move up north to live with her and her family, but I did not want to interrupt my children's lives and felt I needed to rise above circumstances while remaining with my spiritual support system!

When a memory abruptly sneaks up, at times I feel as though it happened just yesterday, even though in reality it occurred twenty-five years ago–though now I can finally admit to myself that it did. I was adamant, though, that I would not remain a victim but would continue to rise above in any way that I could. It became my *spiritual quest*: having faith, strength, endurance, and hope — even on days when I feel numb!

Pathology

This was not the life I had dreamed of — it had always been someone else who experienced tragedies. I had been a Christian believing in love and trusting people in authority, especially doctors. To be systemically seduced and brainwashed can come so quietly into your life that you don't know it happened, perhaps for years; you only know that life has changed. Over the years I was taken in slowly by a sociopath psychiatrist who proved to be an expert in his chosen means of manipulation, exhibiting a deadly mix of narcissism and charisma in order to succeed in his domination of women. In the wake of his sinister practices, I was left with a drastically changed innermost being, personality, and left gathering the devastation of mental and emotional wreckage for many years!

CHAPTER 19

YEAR LATER

Authentic Love

In the summer of 1999, eleven years after the tragic circumstances with Dr. Brady, I had become a spiritual practitioner. I began to implement daily prayers while journaling the kind of man I desired to marry: a family man with faith, values, true love, and who was trustworthy. This was a practice of drawing in one's soul mate and then turning it over to God!

That fall, a gentleman whom I had met at work invited me to lunch. He was a widower with children and grandchildren. Something stirred within me on a higher consciousness level, as though I knew him! I immediately phoned my girlfriend Elizabeth, telling her, "I have just met my soul mate!" We were married three years later, in 2002!

His background was of altruistic love of family, God, and helping others. He gave me a home and hope, but most of all my husband accepted me and my family with open arms! Our beautiful wedding in a chapel on Carlsbad Beach was the most wonderful day of my life, other than giving birth to my children!

A Female Counselor

A few years after my marriage I returned to counseling, as I still had PTSD. It had been fifteen years since I had seen a therapist. At first I visited a group of counselors who were helpful, but feeling that I was on too much medicine, I returned to my family doctor. Then I met Cathy, an MFT who had her own office and was experienced in sexual assault, anxiety, and PTSD. I yearned for completion—Cathy was a beacon of light for me: smart, kind, intuitive, and patient. It took me a couple of years to trust again. Sometimes I would leave for months, not wanting to loose myself. But did come to trust her and work with her.

Cathy helped me realize that although I had done much spiritual work, it still takes time for one's spirit to incorporate itself again, with the body and mind after so much trauma, especially when it is repressed. I came to understand that I had moved on with life spiritually and intellectually, but had not dealt with my assault emotionally, which kept my subconscious mind in turmoil.

A Memoir

A couple of years later after becoming a service minister, I felt a calling to write this memoir, which was written between 2013 and 2017. As I put the catastrophic episodes that had permeated my life back together again, my deeper memory returned. It transpired in layers through journaling, meditation, prayer, and guidance from the Holy Spirit!

As well, with Cathy's support my memories awakened. One morning in 2015 while writing, I had another breakthrough remembering the "freedom" of kneeling down putting my head on Dr. Brady's lap, which I thought was endearing. It was the little girl in me, and the blossoming woman as well. Then fear would surface again as to his deceit.

This is a true story written from my soul and heart, which needed to be accomplished slowly and deeply. Often I felt as though I were coming out of another world. I grew phenomenally, being able to view it objectively, to some degree, which was an aid to my healing and understanding.

Completion

As I was finishing this chapter in April 2017, I suddenly became immersed with dreams of Chad, our sweet love, and the pregnancy from 1980! This went on for about six weeks, making me feel tearful at times. I had couple of nightmares too; one was of me turning around seeing a doctor, begging him to put my baby back inside me. Another was of our families being so happy that I was pregnant, but I had to painfully tell them that my baby had died. I pondered why this was happening now after so many years—my last dream would give me the answer.

The final dream was of a lovely woman in a graceful white wedding dress walking down the aisle with a baby bump. I saw a reflection of myself and Chad, who was waiting for me at the altar. I realized that I had just completed my unfinished grief from thirty years ago, born of the broken engagement and the loss of our baby thirty years ago. I sought help from Dr. Brady for this loss, but instead my life was put on hold when I was thrust into his secret world of sexual assault and brainwashing!

During this chapter I had two more apparitions. The first one was At Easter, which commemorates the rising of the Christ consciousness. A vision of a silver horizontal cross was directly over my husband and me.

Then on Mother's Day as I completed this memoir, another shining silver cross appeared right in front of my eyes. It was a beautiful holy sight to behold of love, acceptance, and faith. I am so grateful to God/Holy Spirit for being beside me on this long journey of discovery, love, healing!

CHAPTER 20

A HEART REMEMBERS

My Beautiful Children

It was a beautiful balmy evening at the resort in the summer of 2015. My husband and I were seated in front of an enormous oak tree with colored lanterns swaying on the branches. We were awaiting the wedding of my son, Sean. My daughter Nadine, as the priestess, was standing happily beside him!

Violins greeted his beautiful bride as she walked gracefully over coral rose petals toward the outside altar. As we rose to honor her, I turned around to view the gathered friends and family all smiling with love on their faces and in their hearts! It was amazing to see some of Nadine and Sean's childhood friends still by their sides! My heart began to flutter, like the feeling I always had when my children were in my womb. Here they were, grown adults sharing one of the most precious moments in all of our lives. I recalled the reason I remained in our small town was to give them strong roots with family and friends.

An enormous healing was taking place for all of us during this touching ceremony, all while we shared our lives and love together. I could not have been more proud of my children seeing how far they had come and how amazing they were. As well, I was beginning to feel that way about myself now. There was a sacred trust of love that we had always shared.

Sean had come up to me before his wedding and asked, "Do I look okay, Mom?"

Smiling, I replied, "Yes, you do, Sean. You look fabulous!"

The day came when he finally told me, "We're good, Mom, we're good!" even asking me to preside over the wedding—but I told him all I really needed to be was just his mother that day.

One day he intimated me that it is the end result in life that mattered, not the past. Today Sean is an outstanding surgeon and wonderful husband. He is also a humble, loving human being. His wife is a real lady and a doctor as well.

Nadine now has two beautiful sons. When she discovered that she was pregnant for the first time she phoned me immediately, announcing, "It wasn't planned, Mom."

"It doesn't matter. Everything will be fine, Nadine: a surprise baby is always special, and I am very happy for you and Andrew," I replied, mentioning her fiancé.

Then she relayed to me that the nurse in the exam room told her she had "other options," but Nadine firmly retorted, "No, I do not!"

"The thought of any abortion is unbearable to me after the years I saw how you suffered, Mom," she confided.

Later I mentioned this to my older sister, who replied, "Anne, you may have saved your grandson's life!"

"Oh, I never thought of it that way, but that makes me happy!"

Nadine is a somatic therapist, priestess, and one of the founders of the Council of Wisdom Women and Sacred Sexuality doing amazing work. She is so filled with love and it resonates through her! My children have made amazing lives for themselves, which is any mother's desire! Over the next couple of weeks after Sean's wedding deeper memory returned, this time recalling those years I had with my children when I was younger. Coincidentally my daughter called to express her love to me, sharing her own memory of me as a loving woman and the wonderful caring mother I was. She also confessed that it took many years before she truly understood the enormous impact on our lives of the secret sexual assault by Dr. Brady.

It was incomprehensible, but we finally saw he fully knew what he was doing. "Mom, I only wish that I could have done something!" she admitted.

"But you were only a child, Nadine—you did not understand!" It's clear she carried much of what happened inside of her as well.

It was through maturity and years of being a mother, therapist, and priestess before she saw the full enormity of my assault! This was divine awareness, it was real, and it would always be there. It outlasted the years that had been stolen from our precious lives together. It rekindled the bond of love I had with my children.

Family Love

My own mother came to mind recently. I understand mental health better now, aided by my own experiences. At times feeling an embodiment of my mother, I feel more compassion for her today. She too had become overdependent, putting her trust in one psychiatrist, Dr. Brady, while placing him on a pedestal!

I still remember all the beauty and love I saw within her: her appreciation of culture, manners, fashion, decorating, and faith. She was gracious and caring to her family as well as numerous others! All of the lovely lullabies she sang to her eight children are imprinted in our hearts! Her daily prayers were her comfort and example of a good life. This love far outweighs any challenges that we all have!

My father too, with his deep Christian faith, was a strong family man who was devoted to his wife and children. No matter what happened, he was there to support all of us. He was an ethical, excellent, and dedicated family physician, well known and respected in our community. He brought love, hope, patience, and faith into his practice without hesitation. He often treated the less fortunate without charge. My years of working with him were my happiest times in a career. He carried that *sacred trust* between doctor and patients always. He knew his role was to promote life, not take it away in any form! He counseled pregnant women and if necessary, would arrange adoptions.

All of my seven brothers and sisters have been a shining light in my life. We learned so much together and supported one another through any crisis, but mostly we had amazing fun times together in so very many ways while discovering the values of sharing, laughter, faith and love! I am so blessed and honored to have come from this large beautiful Catholic family with all of our adventures, quirks, and loving times!

An Ode to My Children
I love you so

Seagulls flying all around us
Catching bread from your little hands
Rolling in the sand with laughter and love
Burying one another and
Building castles to the sky!

The bright colored coral where we
Used to hunt for crabs
Beautiful seashells we gathered in
Our pockets to place on our windowsill
The jewels that we had

Breastfeeding you on the beach
No matter who was there
We didn't care.
Milk baths we took together
Your laughter filled the air
It seemed like it was everywhere.

The pink and purple sunsets
We could see from our duplex
And the never-ending rainbows that came
"From Heaven" I would say!

Driving to the country town of Julian
To cut down our Christmas tree
Stringing popcorn and cranberries

To decorate the evergreen
The year we had "nothing" but
we had everything!
I birthed you but you
Gave me life.

We had each other to love and hold
I sang and rocked you for hours
in my orange rocking chair
While you gazed into my eyes
And pulled my hair.

Our simple dining room we made
With tulip wallpaper and
Golden beads
We sat on colored pillows around
The top of a card table we found
Along the way, the neighborhood
Children would come to play

Jumping off waterfalls in Oregon with
Uncle Mike – how beautiful it was
Around the firelight! Lake Tahoe
Was the starlight of our adventures
With all the family.
We never missed a trip

Cupcakes and cookies we baked
together
While reading books of old
Our secret garden and

"What do children want to know"
I love you so

Your teen years flew by and
Then they were gone
I had to leave you suddenly
With so much going on.
You made it on your own
The wiser I would say.
My daughter you're a therapist
Teaching love in every way.

My son you are such a man
With healing hands and heart.
A physician, like Papa
A beautiful wife and a yacht.
You learned how to live,
You were smart

God gave you both to me
I thank him every day
For life, for happiness
Our memories will grow again
From day to day
As we remember love
Along life's way
I love you so

Loving you always,
Mom

"Family Love"
"Loving Mother of 8 children!"

CHAPTER 21

ENLIGHTENMENT

"Your patients aren't a problem.
They're the reason you exist.
They're a blessing to you."

~ Quote from Georgetown Medical School

A Physician's Prayer

Lord, Thou Great Physician,
I kneel before Thee. Since
Every good and perfect gift
Must come from Thee,
I Pray:
Give skill to my hand, clear
vision to my mind, kindness
and sympathy to my heart.
Give me singleness of purpose,

Strength to lift at least
A part of the burden of my

Suffering fellow men, and a
True realization of the rare
Privilege that is mine, Take
From my heart all guile and
Worldliness, that with the
Simple faith of a child. I may
Rely on Thee. Amen
(A litho in Italy)

Taking advantage of a vulnerable patient is one of the worst things a doctor can do! It makes for such a broken trust that goes to the very core of one's being! The side effects could be that far-ranging that victims often take years to overcome them and return to truth.

Mental Health

Mental health disorder is very common, affecting millions of people as diabetes or thyroid problems do. Awareness has risen greatly over mental illness, instead of just "sweeping it under the carpet." Many are predisposed to it since it is a genetic disorder triggered by any challenges, stress, abuse, or loss. Stated simply, it is a chemical imbalance which affects the brain.

Mental health disorder can set in during the teen years or earlier. Understanding is important in order to seek medical help for your loved one, which can begin with your primary physician. Family intervention may be necessary for support and comprehension of it. Today there are excellent medicines available if needed, along with therapy and purely spiritual practices.

Posttraumatic stress disorder can affect anyone who has been through sexual abuse or other tragedies. It not only occurs among veterans but is also rampant among women, children, or men. It is an extremely serious disorder — now considered an illness — which should be addressed as soon as possible should sexual assault or other forms of abuse are expressly confirmed.

Spiritual Insights

With deeper spiritual awareness, maturity, and balanced mental health, I never would have chosen to have any abortion. It went squarely against my integrity, spirituality, and femininity! My son Sean was conceived after Roe vs. Wade came into effect in 1974, and abortion never even crossed my mind — I can't imagine my life without Sean or Nadine!

But with the meltdown of society and the "new normal" comes a slackening of values, morals, and spiritual truths! Some women are coerced into abortion as though it were a common cold. Others are threatened or even murdered over this beautiful miracle of life — and I was one of them. It doesn't just affect women, it extends to our parents, children, grandparents, and other family members. Abortion not only degrades women but men as well, and often ends relationships! It can affect people for decades!

When medicine has "progressed" to the point of taking lives instead of saving them, it is devastating. There are many doctors who refuse to practice abortion due to their ethics and sticking to the "Hippocratic Oath" they take! Then there are those doctors who stopped performing abortion, unable to continue the inhumane practice. I once had a doctor tell me that abortion is "just another procedure"!

Oh my God, I thought, no it isn't! Not only does it take our babies' lives, it alters the physical, emotional, and spiritual lives of the mother!

Amazing Wise Women

Two lovely women I know were both expecting their fourth babies. The husbands were concerned of having more responsibility with another child. One of the women, unsure of what to do, prayed to God asking to hear her favorite song, "You Are the Wind Beneath My Wings," if God didn't want her to abort. As she sat on the table in the clinic waiting for the doctor, the song began playing in the office—she immediately got up, leaving the clinic! They are still happily married and had their first boy, who is an awesome integral part of the whole family.

The second woman friend realized as she sat in the clinic that she just did not want to have an abortion, no matter what her husband said. She too simply left the clinic. Their baby boy brought much love and happiness to all of their lives; later in his life, he had a set of beautiful twins whom everyone adores while bringing them more love and joy! I commend these women for their inner strength and beauty!

Is It Really a Choice?

There really is not a "choice" for abortion. The sacredness of human life has always been in our creator's hands! As we are becoming more conscious again of our spiritual lives and world, many are drawn to reverse the error made of "Roe vs. Wade."

The beautiful life of an unborn child's conception begins in the Higher realms, beyond our physical being. A mother is the Sacred Vessel to hold and protect this spiritual being. The choice has already been made!

There has been tremendous grief and remorse for many years from the "loss of a child," which I too have experienced and seen in numerous people! Although we cannot turn back the clock, we can move forward into the morals, ethics, and values we once held precious, remembering who really is in charge!

I certainly am not judging as I had many lessons to learn in life myself!

Forgiveness

As my spirit and body finally released the past, I came to my boundaries of self with clarity, and more remembrance of who I used to be returned. Thus I forgave myself for having been vulnerable, naïve, and of having made some poor decisions! And now I can finally forgive Dr. Brady. He too is a child of God, as we all are, and I pray that he has come to truth, love, and peace within his soul.

Although I had lost many growing years of my young adult life, I did finally overcome my assault and grew beyond it. I still need some medication to deter the affects of fear, anxiety, and panic, but I did come to acceptance of my assault as well as the changes it made in my health. The nightmares and flashbacks have dissipated after thirty years.

It is my sincere hope that this true story will help to raise awareness and consciousness of the horrific effects of sexual assault, brainwashing by doctors, or other powerful authority figures!

I never had any more children do the years of recovering and necessary healing. Nadine and Sean, though, have made up for this with their immense love and successful lives!

Love

"You are here for your own transformation and awaking." ~ ACIM

True love first begins within ourselves. It is a feeling and knowing that we follow instinctively. It is your oneness with God and our inborn nature given to us by our Creator. We only have to listen, be in tune, and become aware as we remember that we are individualized expressions of God. This is our guiding light which we can call upon anytime and is always positive. We are in fact spiritual beings having a human experience!

For any seeming difficulty in life, we can remember that there is a Divine Plan. There always is a silver lining to life whatever comes our way. It only takes faith and patience and sometimes persistence. This love is in our hearts and its energy surrounds our lives and extends to others.

Stay true to yourself and you will be given direction and lifted up by love and Spirit! You can heal and you can forgive!

"Remember only the Good." ~ACIM

I continue to have apparitions (visions) of crosses appear to me. I understand that I have been purifying my soul while creating an opening to the Spiritual Realm.

ACKNOWLEDGEMENTS

To God for showing me Heaven, angels, and love! From my heart I would like to honor my father, Dr. Carl Bengs, a deeply devoted and loving physician, husband, father, and grandfather who never lost his integrity or faith in God or for human life! To my loving children, Nadine and "Sean.: who lived through many years of my "torment." Without your beautiful hearts and spirits I'm not sure I would have survived! For my wonderful Irish mother of eight who was a strong and compassionate soul! What faith! I love you Chris and Candy for always being there with open arms for me! Your love of family and others reaches the heavens! April, you are a diamond in the sky! To Dr. John Allen for your never-ending commitment, expertise, and persistence with me — against all odds! I'll never forget you! Cathy, my deepest gratitude for "picking" me up again when I awakened to a deeper reality of my assault. Your beautiful spirit is a healing light! Elizabeth Lennon, my little Scottish "fairy": you always listened to me with utter patience and support —

thank you so much. Peggy, my lovely older sister now in heaven: our hearts are one! To all of my seven siblings: you have brought so much joy, faith, happiness, and fun into our lives together! To my "Course in Miracles" friends who continue to extend love while raising the consciousness of humanity. I so appreciate my husband's family for their big hearts of love and acceptance! Finally, my amazing husband of fifteen years now who never gave up on me but loved me through a process of healing and wholeness: you have given me a beautiful life and are an exemplary man! My love for you is true!

APPENDIX

A Course in Miracles
Resource Center
1-714-632-9005
email:info@miraclecenter.org

Unity Silent Prayer
1-714-632-9005
Unity.org/pray

Victims of Crime -
Report and receive help
victimsofcrimd.org
1-855-484-2846

Medical Board of California
Checks doctor's background
Or report misconduct
Mbc.ca.gov/about us

Natural Science
How to spot a sociopath
Rules for personal empowerment
www.naturalnews.com

PTSD - Sexual assaul against females
RAINN
1-800-656-hope (4673)

Wisdom Women
Counsel Steward of Sacred Sexuality
www.nadinekeller.com

Nadine Keller, MA
Integrative Holistic Practitioner
Mindfulness, Somatic Psychology, Hakomi
Certified Reiki Practitioner Level 1 & 2

Ordained Priestess, Minister and Dakini
Sacred Temple Work, Holy Anointing, Rites of
Passage
Tantra, Couples and Women's Sexuality
Workshops, Retreats & Private Immersions

www.nadinekeller.com
www.ecstatic-awakenings.com

(650) 219- 9395

Founding Member and Council Steward
of Sacred Sexuality with Wisdom Women

181

CPSIA information can be obtained
at www.ICGtesting.com
Printed in the USA
FSHW01n0139280918
52456FS